The Chief Shepherdess

www.penguin.co.uk

The Chief Shepherdess

Lessons in Life, Love and Farming

ZOË COLVILLE

bantam

TRANSWORLD PUBLISHERS
Penguin Random House, One Embassy Gardens,
8 Viaduct Gardens, London SW11 7BW
www.penguin.co.uk

Transworld is part of the Penguin Random House group of companies
whose addresses can be found at global.penguinrandomhouse.com

Penguin
Random House
UK

First published in Great Britain in 2023 by Bantam
an imprint of Transworld Publishers

A CIP catalogue record for this book
is available from the British Library.

ISBN 9781787635746

Typeset in 14/17.5 pt Garamond MT Std by Jouve (UK), Milton Keynes
Printed and bound in Great Britain by Clays Ltd, Elcograf S.p.A.

The authorized representative in the EEA is Penguin Random House Ireland,
Morrison Chambers, 32 Nassau Street, Dublin D02 YH68.

Penguin Random House is committed to a sustainable future
for our business, our readers and our planet. This book is made
from Forest Stewardship Council® certified paper.

To Mum and Dad,
even though I'm still fuming I was never allowed a pet,
to wear hoop earrings or use swear words.
Making up for it now.
Love ya, Zo xx

Contents

Badass Mumma

The pregnant sheep is feebly pushing and pawing the ground. She's tucked herself away in a little wooded patch in the corner of the top field, clearly in distress and close to exhaustion, barely able to stand. I've spotted her on a walkabout to check on the progress of the expectant mums in our flock of 150 Welsh Mountain ewes (fabulous fleeces), Mules (leggy, speckle-faced sheep) and Suffolk Mules (black-faced sheep). As I climb the steep slope yet again, I'm thinking just how peachy my bum is going to get from all the outdoor exercise. Won't be needing my gym membership much longer if I carry on like this! But then I see the sheep and my stomach plummets.

I recognize her – she's a little Welsh Mountain ewe that we call Donkey, although I'm not sure how she got her name. She's small with an arched Roman nose, a soft thick fleece and a long fluffy tail. She's also pretty tame and we've been looking forward to seeing her lamb. But although I'm only a part-time shepherdess, it's obvious something's going badly wrong for her. I grab my mobile and ring Chris – he's my boyfriend, and right now he's definitely the only experienced sheep farmer in our little team of two.

'Okay – what exactly can you see, Zo?' he asks me. As always he stays calm, which helps a lot.

I go around to the business end of Donkey. Protruding out of her rather tight vagina is a swollen lamb's head, tongue hanging out, and a hoof. But for an easy birth, the lamb needs to come out like Superman, two feet and a head.

'Shit, babe,' I say, into my mobile. 'I think her lamb's got stuck. This isn't looking good.'

It is mid-April 2018. Walkers have just launched their lamb-and-mint limited-edition crisps (gone but never forgotten), London is prepping the bunting for the royal wedding of Harry and Meghan, and Twitter is popping off with baked-bean-coloured world leaders tweeting like there's no tomorrow. And I'm no farmer. I'm a hairdresser. Yep – that's right. I work in a salon in Soho, central London, and on holidays and weekends, I come down to Kent to join Chris on the farm. Right now the spring weather's gloriously sunny and I can see for miles across the woods and softly rolling hills of the North Downs. This is the first lambing season I've really embraced, and I've noticed that I'm starting to develop an understanding of sheep's behaviour. That's why Chris now has the confidence to ask me to do check-ups, to make sure everyone has their lambs and no one's in distress or acting peculiarly.

'Can you help her get the lamb out? Can you pull it? Or get it in a better position?' he asks me.

'Erm,' I reply. 'Erm, I need to put the phone down.'

I look at the ewe. It's lucky she's small: I'll be able to hold her comfortably. It's her size that's caused the problem, though – her pelvis is really narrow and unfortunately, by the look of things, she's got a very large lamb. I drape my T-shirt over her head, which I know will help to keep her calm, and kneel down to her in my sports bra and cut-off shorts – quite the Lara Croft look, I think. Except that I'm not really Lara Croft. I'm just extremely out of my depth, half naked and on the verge of a panic attack.

Right, Zoë, I say to myself, sternly. *This girl's in trouble and you have to try to help her.*

I've been watching lambs arrive regularly over the last couple of weeks and, just as Chris said, I know I have two options: to try to manoeuvre the lamb so both its legs come forward as they should, or to give the one foot and head that have emerged a hefty tug and hope the shoulders can make it through the mother's pelvis without causing any damage. There are split seconds for me to make this decision. My heart's racing and I'm dripping with sweat; once I'm committed there'll be no coming back from it. There's a life at stake. I take a very deep breath.

'Okay,' I say to Donkey. 'I'm kind of a novice here but I'm going to do my best. You are a proper badass mumma and you have got this.' I can only hope she finds my words encouraging.

I decide that the best thing to do is to pull. I've seen Chris doing it. I know I need to wait for her next contraction so that we're working together as a team. When I see her tummy clench, I use every muscle in my upper body as I haul at the lamb to try to bring it into the world.

'That's it, darlin',' I tell her. 'Here we go.' My voice is shaking but I try to sound more confident than I feel. 'One last push.'

I instantly realize it's a whole lot harder than Chris made it look. The lamb feels stuck. I quickly use my hand to work around its body, trying to open up the birth canal some more. Nothing's budging. *Shit*. I quickly shift onto my backside on the ground alongside Donkey so that I can brace my legs against a tree – and with that to push against, I can concentrate my force. Suddenly the lamb is moving. Another enormous heave and it slithers out of the ewe, flops onto the ground with a soft little thud and lies still.

My heart nearly stops. Is it dead? It looks a bit like a Simpson, covered in the mustardy-yellow goo of its birth fluids. I remember on another of my weekends down from London, watching Chris swinging a newborn lamb by its back legs to get the mucus and gunk out of its chest to help it breathe. I grab the motionless lamb, which is frighteningly slippery, and scramble to my feet, swinging its little body around like my life depended on it. After a few seconds, I see its chest move, then it sneezes and starts breathing normally. I think it's just a bit stunned by its delivery experience. As am I.

I'm high on adrenalin. Tears are streaming down my face. I pop the lamb on the ground and start frantically rubbing its tiny body. Once it's wriggling, I pull it around to where its mother can see it, to get the ewe-and-lamb bonding going as quickly as possible. I've seen Chris pressing new mothers' heads down to bring them into contact with their offspring, and even smearing birthing fluid onto a sheep's gums when she wasn't showing much interest. Luckily, this ewe starts sniffing, then licking at her lamb. 'No wonder you needed a hand, sweet'eart,' I say to her. 'I wouldn't fancy that coming out of my vagina either.' She gives a throaty little *beeeeh!* and the lamb starts chatting back. *Way to go, Mumma,* I think.

I put the lamb into recovery position – on its tummy, both pairs of legs stretched out to open up its chest and help with breathing. By now I'm feeling like an absolute hero and I'm desperate to tell Chris. I grab my phone with gooey hands.

'Babe? You still there? I did it! It's been born! I think they're bonding now.' A little bit of me is expecting some kind of MBE for my performance but that's not my boyfriend's style.

'That'll do, Pig,' he says to me. It's about the highest praise I ever receive. Still, I can hear that he's pleased. I'm really looking forward to strutting over to him later to show off Donkey and her new lamb. It's an amazing feeling – a real high. Looking back, I can see that this was one of my first moments of questioning whether I'm truly cut out for farming and realizing (as much of a surprise to me as to anyone else) that the answer might be 'Yes.'

The lamb starts getting to its feet while its mother is nuzzling and licking it. I watch proudly, until I spot something else. I thought that the blood-smeared stringy stuff that's hanging underneath the lamb was its umbilical cord: it mostly breaks while lambs are being born so they arrive with it dangling off them. It's usually short and a bit like those kids' sweets called strawberry laces. Except this doesn't look like an umbilical cord. It looks like guts – and quite a lot of them, in fact. Tiny lamb intestines.

Oh, my God. This isn't good. I grab the phone and quickly call Chris back. 'Babe?' I say. I'm really scared now, holding onto my self-control as best I can. 'It's the lamb – I think I've hurt it. Like – burst its belly. I can see guts.'

I feel so guilty.

There are a couple of beats of silence down the line. Chris understands what this means, but I don't get it yet.

'What do I do, babe?' I ask him. 'Can you come over? Shall I call the vet?'

'Right,' Chris says. 'Okay, Zo, I'll drive round. You call the vet.'

When she answers my call, I quickly explain: newborn lamb, ruptured cord. Is there anything she can do?

'Is it clean?' she enquires.

'Clean?'

'Where did you lamb her?'

'Out in the field. So, erm, there's mud, there's bits of grass stuck to it.'

'Right. Okay. We have a couple of options here. You can bring the lamb in if you want, and we can try to stitch the rupture. But the risk of infection is pretty high. It's your call, but I think we need to consider the welfare of the animal.'

I understand what she means. The last thing I want is for the lamb to suffer. I think a part of me had known this already.

'Do you have means to dispatch?' she asks me.

While I'm still talking to the vet, I see Chris at the wheel of the truck coming along the track to where I'm waiting. He parks up and waits until I end the call. I walk over to him, but I can't say anything. From the look on his face, he's known all along what the vet would say. But he also knew I needed to find out for myself that there's no hope. He nods.

Chris always has his gun in the truck. He picks up the newborn lamb and gently carries it around the far side of the vehicle where its mother can't see. There's a pause. I know how much Chris hates having to do this, even when it's the kindest option. He takes a few seconds to compose himself. Then I hear the shot.

'Sorry, babe,' he says, when he comes back. 'But it wouldn't have been fair . . . the bacteria—'

'I know,' I interrupt. And I truly do understand. It just doesn't make it any easier to get my head around.

In this job, I decide if an animal, a conscious, breathing being, lives or dies. My actions are the difference. Most days, life and death overlap. It's the reality of farming. I look across the North Downs, still and peaceful in the hot spring sunshine. The sky is a beautiful clear blue. I can hear bees humming and the soft chattering of birds – the darkness of death interwoven with new life all around me. Instinctively, I know that in order to choose this path, I'll need to find the joy to cancel out the lows.

Can I do it? I wonder. *How will I cope? Can I really live this life?*

Not What I Signed Up For

I don't come from farming stock. That was Chris. We knew each other almost twenty years ago at school in Kent, but while we were growing up nothing happened between us. When I was eighteen, I decided Kent was boring and stale, and far too quiet to fulfil my taste for adventure, so I left for the bright lights and the big city of London to work at a salon in Selfridges on Oxford Street.

Since my early teens, I'd always fancied hairdressing. I loved the creativity and artistry of it, the sociability, too: helping people feel and be the very best they can. I also liked the prospect of mastering a skill. But my grammar school wasn't on board with this idea, so I finished up starting A levels, then dropping out, and finally going to art college. While I was there I spent most of my time in the darkroom, learning about photography. Using historic techniques to capture a singular moment in time was magic to me.

By now I was just that bit older – old enough to stick to my guns about what I really wanted. I trained as a hairdresser, and when I got the Selfridges job, I moved into my then-boyfriend's uni hall just off Brick Lane – which wasn't strictly allowed. A couple sharing a tiny uni room, not to mention an even tinier single bed wasn't ideal and I'm sure contributed to our demise. After a couple of flatshares with friends, which resulted in me finding my feet a little and eventually moving to Stoke Newington in North London, I left Selfridges and took a job in a well-known salon on Beak Street in Soho, called Tommy Guns, to continue my hairdressing career. There was nothing like the buzz of being right in the middle of the city and having a brilliant time. I changed my hair, clothes, and tried lots of different looks: there was the punky phase (white hair with lilac ends, nose ring and fishnets), the flaming-copper pixie-crop with undercut, the Lily Allen phase (big gold hoops, floral dress and trainers). I was experimenting, wanting to find out which of them was me.

I must have seemed confident, but that wasn't quite how I felt. As a little girl, I'd always wanted to perform on a stage: I loved the limelight, and hoped with all my might to be cast as Mary in the school Christmas nativity play (sadly, I never was), or be chosen to write on the blackboard. I spent most nights fantasizing about the day I could wear 'clip-clop' shoes with heels and be the focus of all eyes. I don't think it was just showing off – there was a bit of insecurity too. Perhaps it was a need for re-assurance, and that was how I felt about falling in love too. I imagined having one human being who was mine and who focused their full attention on me – always. Except, of course, I know now what I didn't know back then: that is a very immature idea of what love really is.

By the time I'd had a couple of relationships, I'd dis-covered that the ideas about romance that I'd had when I was little – listening to a borrowed copy of J.Lo's *This Is Me. . . Then* CD and spritzing my diary with Charlie Red scent – weren't realistic. The type of man I was attracted to wasn't the foot-massage-and-kisses-on-the-cheek-in-Waitrose type anyway. I was more likely to fall for a cheeky (but clumsy) bum grab in Lidl. Well, you have to be realistic, don't you? I also had parents who were still together and still happy, which not everybody does, and for that I'm very thankful. Mum and Dad still held hands and he bought her grown-up knickers for Christmas. On the whole, he was pretty much a perfect model of how to be happily married and what I should look for in a man.

When Chris and I got back in touch, a few years had gone by. Our reunion happened thanks to Facebook Messenger: a ping at 1 a.m., and the screen light woke me up. *To be fair*, the message read, *you are gorgeous. X.* A glance at the name told me it was 'little Chris' from hazy house parties back when we were at school. I'd noticed him liking my photos from a recent holiday in Crete, and the odd status here and there, clearly psyching himself up to start a conversation with me. What a way to introduce yourself. I typed back, *Wow, romance really is dead*, rolled over and fell back to sleep. The next morning, he explained that he'd had a few sherbets and apologized. But he wasn't giving up, and after that he pursued me via Messenger until the early hours every single night. Back then, he was a plumber in South London, commuting every day through the dreaded traffic blackspot near the Blackwall Tunnel.

Until his parents' divorce, Chris had been a farm child. After they broke up, he chose to spend his free time there – the farm was where he felt most himself and where he wanted to be. But then his dad was diagnosed with a brain tumour and when Chris was twelve, he died. Chris went to live full-time with his mum, who did her best, but he had to watch all the animals be taken away, which was heartbreaking. He was left with just his Jack Russell. Benny had been a present from his dad and the two of them were inseparable. Later, Chris responded to the upheaval, understandably, by setting out to make himself as financially secure as possible. He even bought a house to do up. He wasn't sure what he really wanted to do with his life but he knew it was important to be the one in charge, not controlled by other people's decisions.

Our first date was a car crash. Frankly, I'm surprised

there was a second. What happened could have killed romance stone dead. I had given in to the Facebook Messenger chase and we arranged for him to come up to Stoke Newington one Saturday evening. He was very busy and running late and I hadn't eaten all day as I'd been so busy in the salon. With that and a longer wait for him than I'd expected, I was half-cut by the time he arrived. He smelt good, had a pair of his best pants and a tooth-brush in his coat pocket and his hands were rough. (Not everybody's type – but mine for sure.) So far, so good.

Out we went. Rum and Coke and more rum and Coke, and before too long we'd met this couple who were teaching us to jive. I really thought I was handling myself spec-tacularly until we went outside for a cigarette and the cold air hit me like a train. 'Will you take me home?' I asked Chris. And he did. He walked me back, used my key to let us in, and as we entered my room, I took off my clothes, not seductively or expectantly, just very aware that I might be sick at any moment, and my high-waisted mom jeans were making my churning stomach feel ten times worse.

He looked at me uneasily. 'Babe,' he said, 'I think you should go to the toilet.' Too late. I projectile-vomited my way down the stairs and redecorated the bathroom with brownish sick. Note to the wise: don't drink on an empty stomach, and especially not on a first date!

I usually did everything I could to avoid vomiting because I had a severe phobia about it. (Chris didn't know that yet – deep psychological issues and hang-ups are hardly a first-date topic of conversation.) As I stood over the toilet in a skimpy bra and knickers, he appeared next to me and handed me a glass of water even though I'd commanded him to stay upstairs.

'How do you look that fit when you're gwebbing?' he wondered.

I was mortified, absolutely mortified, but don't remember much else until I woke up under the duvet with a mouth like Gandhi's flip-flop. I rolled over to see Chris lying on top of the duvet fully dressed, including a belt. Subsequently I found out he'd been freezing and desperate for a wee all night but he didn't want me to think he had taken advantage and he couldn't remember where the bathroom was. What a gent.

From then on, we steadily dated. Although we were in a brand-new relationship, there was also an air of nostalgia as he was close to the boys I'd grown up with. I started going down to stay with him at weekends, and now, instead of Kent being a dull Dark Ages place I'd been keen to leave behind, I found my visits comforting. I enjoyed being back where he and I had grown up, going out for brunches in country pubs and taking trips to the beach. I'd sit in the train getting butterflies at the thought of seeing him again – the sort of flutters where you aren't sure if a nervous poo could be on the agenda and you bloody hope it's not. Our relationship blossomed. I'd get the train on a Saturday night and he'd come and pick me up from the station covered with dust and dirt in his white Ford Transit van. I remember how he'd shout, 'Oi oi, darlin'!' from the wound-down window as soon as my foot touched the platform.

Three months in, things suddenly got serious between us – just not in a good way. Not long before we'd started dating, Chris had been travelling in Asia on the classic backpackers' trip, with hostels, insanely cheap booze and carefree living. Until he had a near-death experience. It happened in Hanoi, Vietnam, where he got infected with dengue fever, a very nasty virus carried by mosquitoes. It's a haemorrhagic fever, which basically means bleeding from every orifice. The nurse administering the IV line in the hospital explained to him in broken English that there was a fair chance he wouldn't survive the night (just imagine the trauma). Although he was practically in shock, he responded very calmly (which I've seen him do at other times of crisis), recording his will on his iPad and trying to accept that this could be the end, in grotty sheets, all alone.

Chris managed to survive that night, and the next, but he knew it had been a close call and it really shook him up. He headed back to England, where his GP advised him to rest as his body had taken such a battering. He moved in with his mum and stepdad for a bit of extra support.

A few months later, we started dating. Perhaps it wasn't the best timing, but he must have thought he was on the road to recovery. All of a sudden, his body shut down, forcing him to stop in his tracks. This literally happened in the street right in front of me. We'd been for brunch in a Stoke Newington hipster café and were planning to go and see the new baby sloths at London Zoo, but suddenly Chris was squatting on the pavement with his head in his hands, sweating profusely. It was his first ever panic attack – terrifying enough just to watch, so it must have been a hundred times worse to go through it. It turned out that his body was telling him – well, screaming at him, really – 'Enough is enough, mate! I'm calling it a day! You've ignored all the warnings and you just won't slow down, so I'm forcing you to stop!'

The whole thing was so frightening – and, worst of all, he didn't bounce back from it. That day was the start of a horrible year when he lay in his room staring blankly through the television, desperate to get better or even scrape together enough energy to hold a conversation when I came to visit him from London. He had to give up his job. His mum and stepdad were kind and supportive but, like all of us, bewildered and unsure how to help. He kept the blinds shut all day because the light was so painful and he told me that his blood felt like 'acid', as though his body was burning and poisoning him from the inside. But he couldn't get a medical diagnosis (his blood tests, said the doctors, were all clear so there was nothing really wrong with him). After a while, he got sick of being told he was likely to be suffering from depression. We were certain something was seriously medically wrong. The problem was the tests just didn't show it.

We did a lot of reading and spent time in online

forums, and after a while, we diagnosed him with ME, or chronic fatigue syndrome. Next, we tried everything to reset his immune system so it wouldn't continue to fight itself and he could get his life back. I put him on alkaline diets and vitamin programmes. He drank colloidal silver – which some of the forums said can help to fight infections – and did clay cleanses to detox . . . He was really open-minded about all of it because he was so desperate to find an answer. Nine months into the nightmare, we borrowed some money to see a private rheumatologist and the outcome was, yes, he did have a form of ME, but the term is so broad that the rheumatologist couldn't pinpoint it exactly. The virus that had triggered off the problem – whatever it was – had rewired his body, and the advice was to 'see how it goes'. That was very hard to accept when he'd lost his old life completely and it seemed that parts of his personality would be altered for ever. As a boy, Chris had had to learn to be resilient, and I saw this quality now.

We'd only been dating a few months when the illness hit us, so we felt a bit hijacked. We'd replaced romantic meals out with picnic teas in bed and made do without weekend trips to Paris. It was different – but we could still have fun together. The way I saw it, camping in the New Forest and ice skating at the Natural History Museum would be pointless if he ended up suffering for weeks afterwards. So, I'd come down from London on a Saturday night and lie with him in silence, making him swallow the alternative medical potions I'd read about and massaging his legs, which were in agony, telling myself it would all be worth it in the end.

Chris's confidence took a tremendous knock. He was grieving for his previous capabilities and felt he was letting me down. He kept telling me forlornly, 'This isn't what you signed up for.'

We decided that he needed a dog. (Every single person needs a dog, in my opinion.) Benny, Chris's childhood dog, wasn't around any more but he'd been a real anchor to Chris when he was a boy, and having someone rely on him might help him to find his feet again. Enter Indie, a black-and-white Springer Spaniel.

She was a tiny ball of sass when she first arrived and I couldn't believe how cute she was, or that from now on I'd be able to smell her tiny ears whenever I wanted to. That first night of motherhood was a rollercoaster. I thought she should definitely stay in her own bed – *Dogs need boundaries! Don't give in when she cries or you'll end up putty in her paws* – but I just couldn't handle her crying and by now Chris was asleep. He'd been suffering from insomnia and I'd learned – unless the house was burning down – not to wake him. I lifted Indie onto our bed and she instantly snuggled under the covers with me – the world's smallest spoon. Our weekends were spent training her and before too long we had her stopping and turning on just a whistle – it was beautiful to watch her work like that. I'd never spent much time around dogs before so I wasn't used to the bond that formed between us. I began to love her unconditionally.

One day when she was still a tiny puppy, we took her to a Wren Kitchens showroom and she started to squat on one of the pretend bathroom floors. This startled Chris so much that he scooped her up in one hand and we hastily travelled back down the escalator to the ground floor. We wanted to get her outside before she started pooing but her little poos were bouncing down the steps like Maltesers. Indie, of course, was completely oblivious. We still joke that she must be on Wren Kitchens' banned list, and if we ever try to take her in there again, we'll be met by uniformed security. That was when we realized she was going to be quite a character.

* * *

I noticed that training her was giving Chris a new focus, and when he started to take her on pheasant shoots, it put him back in touch with some of his dad's old friends. He even dug out his dad's tweed jacket and started wearing it. That was one major difference between us: I wasn't allowed to watch *Jurassic Park* as a kid because it was too scary, while he was learning to fire a gun! The shoots felt like rebuilding a link between father and son, which seemed to help Chris's mental health and supported his recovery.

It was around this time that he started chatting with his dad's best mate, Ian, who offered him some farm work.

Chris began to go up to Ian's place to help him sort sheep into different groups for winter grazing or to be taken to market. Farming lingo crept in more and more often as we chatted, and it was pretty emotional to hear all his memories of his dad and old childhood stories.

Very early on, we also had a real scare. Looking back, it was a sign of what was coming: a glimpse into a world where you can't spend too much time worrying about the might-have-beens because you don't control them and that's just the way it is. Chris was going on a shoot between Christmas and New Year and he asked if Indie should come with him that day or be left at home with me. 'Aw, let her stay here,' I said. 'She can keep me company.'

That casual decision saved her life when one of the other shooters made a very bad misjudgement. Instead of firing up into the air, he aimed downwards, showering Chris's legs with pellets. If Indie had been standing alongside him on the lead, she'd have been killed. When Chris rang me, he was playing things down.

'Don't tell my mum, Zo, but there's been a bit of an accident.'

'What kind of accident?'

'Well – I've been shot.'

I was aghast, but he kept insisting that I mustn't say anything. 'I'm fine, babe. The guy who screwed up with the gun, he's driven me to the hospital.'

I felt better as soon as I knew he was going to be okay, but those awful what-ifs can completely take over your thoughts when you realize you've just dodged a major disaster. In the end, the doctors made him stay in overnight, so I had to tell his family even though he didn't want me to, and we all drove over to see him. At first they were saying he might need an operation to get the shotgun pellets out of his knees, but then the surgeon decided that that would be so invasive it was best to leave the pellets to work their own way out. (Chris had a follow-up surgical procedure months later.) For now, all they could do was to pick as many of them out as they could out with tweezers, and by the time I got there, Chris was as high as a kite on pain medication. They'd told him that his neoprene wellies had saved his legs by absorbing the impact: those posh farming boots had made all the difference.

* * *

'Babe?' I heard Chris's voice down the phone one day in the salon. 'So . . . I may or may not just have bought a pen of Suffolk Mules.'

I stared out of the window of the salon into Beak Street where a serious pair of trainers was just strutting past. *Ooooh. Limited edition Nikes.*

'What the hell's a Suffolk Mule?' I enquired.

'They're sheep,' he said.

'And how many sheep have you bought?'

'Thirty-two.'

Well – at least that doesn't sound too many.

'O*kaaay* . . . so where exactly are you planning to keep them?'

It turned out he'd also rented a field. When I saw the Suffolk Mules the following weekend, I discovered that thirty-two sheep *did* look like quite a lot after all, but I could tell how excited Chris was. (They turned out to be a breed with a black face and legs and white fleece, and they were soon to multiply: the whole lot were in lamb and due in a matter of months.) But after all he'd been through, if this was what it took to bring happiness and purpose back into his life and help him on the road to recovery, I was happy for him. After all, I thought at the time, it would never be more than a hobby.

The way I see it now, Chris never really chose to take up farming: he fell back into it as though he'd never left. This world was familiar and soothed him at a time when he felt like he'd lost everything. I also think it helped him to get stronger again, both mentally and physic-ally. Subconsciously, he knew so much without being taught and I could see this old knowledge resurfacing as I watched him interacting with animals. He was so in tune with them and their movements that he could pre-dict which way they'd run before they did. Meanwhile, for me, there was a lot to take in. I knew nothing about anything – the terminology, the etiquette, all of it was strange. Damn it, I couldn't even whistle! It was going to take some dedication to learn how to behave around these animals: where to stand, how to stand, what noises to make and what noises to avoid. Exciting for sure, but daunting too.

I was also learning more and more about Chris, and exactly how different our upbringing had been. It's extraordinary that we're in a functioning relationship, really. He'd spent his boyhood weekends running errands in his dad's livestock lorry with his pet chick on his shoulder – its name was Chickie and he'd hatched it himself in an incubator he'd got as a birthday present. Meanwhile, I'd spent parts of my childhood in my dad's Nissan Bluebird, reading *Harry Potter* books and visiting National Trust properties in my Spiceworld fluorescent crop top.

Auctioneers at the livestock market used to let eight-year-old Chris bid and buy all sorts of animals because they knew his dad wouldn't mind, and there I was, with an imaginary puppy called Toffee that I used to drag around wherever I went. One thing was for sure: once he was visiting the livestock market on a Tuesday again, leaning on the pens his dad would have leaned on, eating a greasy full English at the same table they'd sat at together, that first bid for Suffolk Mules was pretty much inevitable.

So I started off dating a plumber and now I was standing in a field, watching him rounding up his sheep. (I was even allowed to have a go.) I could see he felt alive, and he hadn't looked that way for far too long. I was happy for him. As for me, my shepherding anecdotes were great fun at the salon, even though not everyone believed I was *really* spending my weekends on a farm. I could see in their faces that many of my clients couldn't place me in that life, and I understood why. At that point, to be honest, I couldn't place myself in it either.

Wild as the Hills

'Fetch 'em in, then, Chief Shepherdess!' yelled Chris.

We were gathering in the wild ewes. The clue's in the name. What a bunch of feral beasts they are. As a good rule of thumb, if the sheep has horns it's going to be a pain in your arse. And, boy did you need a bloody good sheepdog – but all we had was the two of us plus Indie. Indie's hard as iron: she doesn't mind bad weather, just wants to get out there and work, and Chris has trained her brilliantly to respond to different whistles and arm movements. These days, she's a proper farming dog. But back then, she and I were very much learning the ropes.

She had to stay in the truck – which left it up to me to round up the sheep.

Chris – the king of nicknames – had crowned me 'Chief Shepherdess' early on in our escapades. He meant it in a light-hearted, encouraging manner, but I'm pretty sure he was also thinking that helping him out in the fields was just a fad for me. How serious could a hairdresser really be about the shepherding game? 'Chief Shepherdess' was just a private joke between the two of us. I guess it escalated a tad.

I'd come straight from the salon that day in a little cotton smock dress with a Bardot neckline (*very Kate Moss at Glasto*, I thought, as I'd finished off the look with my wellies). At this point there were some areas of life I definitely wanted to keep control over, and my wardrobe was one of them. So long as I still bore a vague resemblance to the old Zoë, I didn't feel like I was losing my whole identity in one hit.

The grass was soaking wet and slippery, and the wild ewes showed zero inclination to go towards their pen. Many breeds of sheep like to flock together and will move as a group if you approach them and drive them forward – but not these. They'd rather scatter. They'll even burrow under fences and squeeze through hedges into spaces where you'd never think they'd fit. I tried a whistle and an arm wave, but despite my best efforts, they dashed off in a dozen directions, running rings round me.

'Why aren't they flocking?' I muttered.

'Jump, Zo!' Chris shouted encouragingly. I knew what he meant – I'd seen him leaping around and whistling, directing the sheep with his arms. But I felt properly stupid when I tried to do it. Then one of them suddenly made a dash for it, springing over the fence into the next field as effortlessly as a gazelle.

Shit. What do I do? Do I go and fetch her back? I hastily scrambled after her. One foot on the wire, whip the leg over – and then I felt a sudden stabbing pain. A sharp line of barbed wire ran along the top of the fence and one of its spikes was embedded in my inner thigh. An inch shy of my knicker line, may I add. *Ouch. For fuck's sake, that was a close shave!* I extricated myself carefully and clambered over. Lesson One: *Don't wear cute little dresses when you're climbing a fence.* I looked across at Chris, who was grinning as he watched all this unfold.

Lesson Two – and this was a big one: *There's no such thing as bad weather in farming, only the wrong choice of clothing.* To start with, I didn't want to invest hundreds of pounds in a hobby I might give up after a few months, so I'd dug out the wellies I'd had since a messy Reading Festival in my teens. What a faux pas that was. After Chris's near-miss when his wellies had saved him from serious injury, perhaps I should have known that there's a very good reason why generations of farmers have all sported the same – expensive – brand of boots. It wasn't long before I was plagued with agonizing chilblains – multiple sores on every single toe. The pain was tolerable as long as my feet stayed cold, but as soon as they warmed up, an indescribable burning/itching sensation would take hold and I'd be chatting to Chris in the kitchen in the evening, ferociously rubbing my feet like a crazed person.

I tried everything Google told me to do to make my chilblains better – I even peed on them while standing in the shower because my grandma swore by it – but nothing worked. The itching was so bad that I had to stop the car, pull off my wellies and my triple layers of socks just to scratch. So I caved and bought a pair of posh boots. I would've spent the same amount of cash on a night out drinking without a second thought . . . but this felt different. Extravagant. I hadn't quite admitted to myself at this point that I *might* end up wearing them every single day.

What else did I need? I looked around the livestock market to find out what was trending. Checked shirt – tick. Fleece gilet – tick. Jeans – tick. Posh wellies or boots – tick. But after that: *Houston, we have a problem.* What about a farmer who sports childbearing hips? She'll be needing waterproofs that don't give her camel toe or quickly develop a saggy arse, and there needs to be room for a pair. It's all too common for overalls not to account for lady bumps, so the minute I pulled them on, the crotch rose and I was at risk of a chronic case of thrush. And how about making that stuff flattering? How hard would it be? Cinched in at the waist – but not so much that you can't fit a hoodie underneath. Shaped enough round the arse to see the faintest outline of a peach – but you don't want them splitting when you jump over a gate.

My new wardrobe staples weren't from glossy shops on Oxford Street. They were overalls that don't rip on the crotch in a week, thermal base layers that don't go bobbly in the tumble-dryer and a waterproof jacket that has enough pockets for all the castration rings, needles and baler twine I could dream of. I suddenly felt like my dad, whose fashion sense was always practical, buying three pairs of the same trousers in case they stopped making them. Once I've found an item that works, I'll keep using it to the bitter end, then replace it with the exact same thing.

I also noticed – especially in springtime – that everyone was so exhausted from lambing, they all got stuck in a cycle of wearing the same outfit day in and day out, with maybe a fleece they'd got for free from a supplier for good measure. No shade here: having now lived through multiple lambing seasons, I know whatever's clean and at the top of the pile when I squint across the bedroom at 4 a.m. is what gets worn. It's not about fashion any more. When your working conditions can be pretty savage and each morning you aren't sure if you're facing an eight- or fifteen-hour day, you need to cater for all eventualities. And if the worst comes to the worst, your spare dry outfit on the back seat of the truck will double as a blanket for a sick lamb.

Lesson Three: *Always shut the gate!* To 'normal' people,

it's not the end of the world to leave the odd gate open or loosely tied. But there have been moments in my relationship with Chris when I've thought my time on Earth is done because I left a gate open. The first time it happened, we were moving five rams from one field to another, making sure they stayed apart from the ewes until the girls were good and ready. The rams were a mixed-breed group, a real bunch of characters, but all of them had that geezer-walk: a straddle-legged, balls-swinging gait. The plan was to follow behind them, nice and steady, and they'd go straight up the track into the field that was waiting. But they didn't. The second they were out, they turned left. *Shit.* Chris and I looked at each other.

'Okay, babe,' he said. 'I'll get ahead and drive them back to you.' Sounded like a plan – but when he tried to sneak up beside them, all it did was speed the rams up. Instead of geezer-walking, they were going at a gallop right along the track. That was when I remembered I'd left the gate wide open. *Shit shit shit.* They thundered on down the road into the village – us racing in pursuit – and vanished up the driveway of a really lovely house. It looked like the owners had spent a fortune on their lawn, which, by the time we got there, had been ploughed up by twenty heavy hoofs. Then one of the rams decided he should leave a memento and took a dump right in the middle. Finally Chris and I managed to get around the back of them as quietly as possible, whispering to each other ('Head 'em off, Zo!' he kept hissing), and we watched them trotting back down the drive with a big sigh of relief.

My second gate-related disaster was on a grander scale. On a blistering hot day, we'd spent over an hour manoeuvring a flock of two hundred ewes out of a field and towards their new pen. We were tired and sweaty – and then one rebel girl decided she had different ideas: she wanted to go back into the field. With sheep, that's all it takes: if one busts out, they all go. Everybody followed. I hadn't shut the gate and we were back at square one. Actually, it was worse than that: once sheep know your plan they get surprisingly clued-up and won't cooperate the second time around. The only thing to do at that point is to move the metal fences and rebuild their whole pen somewhere else.

It was an epic fuck-up on my part. I still had one foot in the salon and I was pretty much all over the place. But the worst thing about what I'd done was that Chris didn't shout and curse at me for being stupid. He didn't even mutter under his breath. What's worse than anger? Disappointment. I could see it. A swift turn on his heels and before I knew it, he was driving away in the truck. He couldn't even look at me, and I felt so guilty. *Gonna have to do better than this*, I thought.

The 'shut the gate' rule goes for footpath walkers also. It may not seem like a big deal but livestock on the road could cause an accident. Teenage pregnancies for heifers are another result of gates being left open, and if you've got a group of female cows even two fields away, whatever their age, they're fresh meat for horny bulls. The females will have been strategically placed in separate fields by the farmer to stop this happening . . . but if a gate is left open, you never know what mischief the bulls will get up to in his or her absence.

But you can't force people to shut gates. You can't stop sheep getting caught in brambles. You can't make it rain. You can't even plan what price you'll get for your animals at the market. I was starting to see just how stark the differences were between the world of farming and my life as a hairdresser, where my days were planned months in advance. The sheer uncertainty would take some getting used to.

Lesson Four: *Keep up with your anti-tetanus jabs.* I was ever so surprised at how quickly I was working as a vet on the farm, learning about antibiotics and how to give injections. It's pretty easy, in fact – at least until the sheep misbehaves.

A little Hebridean – a petite breed of sheep with horns – had been attacked by a dog. To recover, she needed antibiotics to stop the bites becoming infected, plus pain relief. She was doing well and I was chuffed with the way I'd learned to position her for her injections by turning her horns like handlebars to push her down towards the ground. Then I got a bit too confident: instead of waiting until she was ready, I thought I'd take the cap off the needle and hold it in my hand as I grasped her horns. She gave a sudden twist, I let go and the needle drove straight into my kneecap. I felt it hit the bone. Chris made sure I squeezed as much blood as possible from the wound in case infection was present, so that was yet another vital – albeit very painful – lesson learned.

Sheep, as I was finding out, are a challenge. The secret is to work *with* them, using their natural behaviour so you don't end up exerting more physical effort than you have to. Slowly, I picked up little tricks – like knowing how much they like to flock and run along fence lines (especially if they think they're escaping). That knowledge is worth its weight in gold. It especially helps because Chris and I are underdogs as shepherds: we don't have expensive quad bikes or tractors, and the equipment we use tends to be on its last legs, which makes even simple tasks, such as rounding up sheep, far harder. It's all we've ever known, so we try not to let it faze us too much. *You don't know you've got it good unless you've had it hard* – as Chris reminds me when I'm using a bucket to transfer a ton of cattle grub from the back of the trailer by hand because we don't have a tractor with a scoop. My biceps and my triceps say, 'Thank you.' It's Reason Number 247 why farmers don't need gym memberships.

* * *

The first few times I tagged along to the livestock market with Chris, the place completely floored me. It's a *very* masculine environment. And these men had lived and breathed farming all their lives. As I walked up the concrete steps towards the pens, I'd suddenly feel really self-conscious, uncomfortable and totally out of place. No one did anything to make me feel that way: the feeling came from me. Looking back, I can see I was far more likely to be judged for my appearance when I was walking down Carnaby Street, but that's not how it seemed at the time. Back in Soho, when I'd rock up to photoshoots for big magazines to assist the hair team, it didn't matter if Joanna Lumley was sitting in that chair, I'd feel carefree and confident. I knew that this was my domain. The livestock market wasn't.

The out-of-place feeling didn't change in just one day, but I remember the turning point so clearly. It was the day I saw another woman of my age. That's pretty rare in itself, but this one had a baby in a sling. Trying hard not to stare, I watched her casually leaning on the metal gate like a total queen. To this day, I still don't know her name but, without so much as saying a word to me, she gave me the confidence to continue going forward. If she belonged in this world, then so could I.

Gradually I found that I could walk from one end of the pens to the other, climbing various gates along the way without feeling everyone's eyes burning into the back of my head. Instead of shying away and flushing when one of the old boys commented on whether my jean shorts were half price as there was only half of them, I'd think of a witty comeback and take it for what it was – two of us from different generations, walks of life and different sexes, in a greasy café queue just waiting to be served. What we had in common was far bigger than our differences.

There was friendly and helpful advice available in the market too, and one day when I mentioned to Chris that a calf in the auction ring was probably stressed (he had 'scours' – diarrhoea) an old boy sitting alongside us who'd overheard me growled, 'You know what will fix that? Feed 'em an egg – shell and all!' and this piece of wisdom just stuck in my mind. I'd never have believed I could feel more myself standing ringside chatting about 'broken-mouthed ewes' on a Tuesday than I would have felt at a bar in Shoreditch sinking tequilas. But, eventually, I did.

* * *

And what exactly is a broken-mouthed ewe? My mind was running away with me thinking of fractured jaws, but really it's when they get older and they start to lose teeth. To start with, learning farming lingo was a ginormous task that I really wasn't prepared for. Chris had heard terms like 'two-tooth' and 'hogget' while he was still in the womb, and he never had to ask what a heifer was. The best way for me to learn all of this was to sit on the pens in the market and earwig. I quickly started picking up some slang, but it took me a while before I was brave and confident enough to say it out loud in public.

The UK has more than sixty different breeds of sheep. I don't think I know half of them yet, even though I've tried really hard. When I first started frequenting the market, after we'd eaten the obligatory bacon and hash brown bap with cheap ketchup, and before the auctions started, Chris and I would look inside every single pen so that he could test me on the breed. It was invigorating to learn something so completely new. We also had a *very* eclectic selection of sheep at home, which helped. He'd point at a random ewe in a field and put me on the spot to name the breed.

At this point, I'd seriously started to regret choosing gymnastics over playing rugby at secondary school: some tackling experience would have stood me in great stead for sheep-wrangling. I'm around five foot four and under 50 kilos, and it's quite daunting to handle something that can easily weigh more than I do. I just didn't have the speed, even when the animal was lame – I could even be outrun by a three-legged sheep. It was quite degrading. I found out that perseverance is key: keep going, wear them down, and when they're flagging, dig deep and find one last surge of energy.

But it's not a natural instinct to launch yourself onto a woolly object moving at speed, and it takes practice to ignore your brain's objections. There's a reason it objects – mess up and you can really get hurt. Even once

you've grabbed her, the ewe will keep bucking and struggling to get away while you grimly hold on and she drags
you along the ground.

The first sheep we ever bought, and therefore the
breed I could recognize first, were those pregnant Suffolk
Mules. We kept them in the first small rented field with
two glute-engaging hills, no shelter and no plumbed-in
water troughs. Chris was still driving the huge white Transit van he'd used for his plumbing jobs – which meant he
sank into the mud the minute it rained – and I was still
working at the salon as my full-time job and therefore
pretty useless at anything sheep-related. He had bought
the Suffolks not long before they were due to lamb, so
there wasn't much time to get in the groove before the
toughest and most exhilarating time of the entire year:
lambing.

Our very first lambing, in February 2017, was a learning curve for sure – a huge test of how far Chris had
come with his recovery from his autoimmune condition.
He was still unwell, but the adrenalin of this new life and
the way that living creatures depended on him was a huge
push to his recovery. I was busy working full-time, not
always able to help, but thankfully, all thirty-two girls were
easy lambers and we didn't have to handle any orphan-
lamb adoptions. I watched my first lamb being born at
sunset on the hill, and assisted in my first delivery there
too. It might sound magical, and in some way it was, but
really it was me with shaky hands and a dry mouth, getting

shouted at by Chris for not taking my rings off. (I was still wearing acrylic nail extensions too, but not for much longer. There's only a certain number of times you can scrape sheep shit from under your fingernails before you decide to give the manicures a miss.)

I definitely got a buzz from seeing that lamb take its first breath up close, and watching the mother and offspring bond as they chatted away to each other. But I didn't rush home and start ordering a shepherd's crook and overalls, that's for sure. Turning your whole world upside down is a very big deal, and I just wasn't quite ready to do it.

* * *

'Hi, gorgeous!' It was Chris. I was out for a boozy Saturday brunch with the girls, and two mimosas down, when the phone rang. 'You're gonna love me! I've got a surprise on board the trailer for you. Except – I think they might be die-ers.'

Die-ers? Who said romance is dead? He'd started bringing me half-dead lambs scooped up in a bucket during lambing season, or buying me a straggler from the market that no one wanted to bid for. And although I had no qualifications for it on paper – I still don't – I was getting more confident about my skills in 'mending' sick animals. There's no buzz quite like watching a die-er – an animal that didn't seem to have much of a chance – out grazing in the sun, fit as a flea. Or, better still, when a comatose lamb sucks from a bottle for the first time. I live for that feeling. Watching a sick animal turn a corner and grow stronger and stronger is a better ego boost than just about anything else I can think of.

Fred and George Weasley were my very first patients: eleven days old, they looked like they were about to collapse at any moment. They were twin ginger calves, Guernseys, a dairy breed that tends to be bonier than beef cattle. But these two could have fallen to the ground if I blew on them too hard. Being boys, they weren't needed on the dairy farm where they were born, so they'd been sent to the market with a bunch of others and bought by Chris.

I had about a million butterflies in my stomach as I rushed to Lidl to get some baby sterilizer, a whisk and a jug. Then I set about disinfecting the milk bar: a calf-feeding unit that looks like a trough with separate bowls and then a teat similar to the mother's corresponding to each bowl. The calves all stand in a line on their teats with their tails waggling uncontrollably. Once it was ready to go, I made a clean pen for the new boys.

The first two weeks they were around, I was certain they would die at any minute. I spent as much time on the farm as I could spare to nurse them. They were too weak to latch onto the milk bar so I had to let them slurp their milk out of a bucket for a few days – not ideal for their digestive system, their 'rumen', but as long as they were getting some kind of nourishment, I crossed my fingers and carried on. By now I was fully invested. I'd given them so much.

A couple of weeks later, when they were growing stronger, I went to help a friend with her wedding hair. I drank plenty of champagne and had a wonderful time. When I got back to the farm, I didn't bother getting changed – just kicked off my shoes, slid my bare feet into my wellingtons and headed for the barn to check on the calves. I'd only been in there for two minutes when Fred shat down the side of my leg, straight into my boot. There's nothing like the squelch of a cowpat round your toes to sober you up fast.

The Weasley calves once ate something they shouldn't have while out grazing and didn't eat, drink or move for two days. Calves' digestive systems can be really sensitive, especially if they're a bit sickly or didn't have a great start in life. For the Weasleys this incident was such a bad case of 'korma butt' that I was convinced they were going to die of a bacterial infection. ('Korma butt' tells you all you need to know about the colour of it: when young livestock are mainly on milk, their poos are yellowy and should be a Mr. Whippy ice-cream texture.) Luckily the lads were still well enough to drink from the teats on the milk bar, so I tried the egg trick I'd been given at the market and gave them both one – shell and all – to bind their gut. Within two days their poos were back to Mr.

Whippys. Cheers to the old boy at the market who was kind enough to pass on that piece of knowledge.

Fred and George were summer calves, which meant I could watch them in the sunshine, enjoying them as they gradually grew stronger. And I knew that they had this chance at life because I had believed in them and worked to make it happen. It really did feel good.

* * *

'How big are his bollocks?' I asked, trying to sound confident.

'Would you like to cup them?' came the reply.

It was market day. Once upon a time, my shopping trips had begun with brunch, including a pancake stack and a few bellinis, and ended with marks on my arms from all the bags while the soles of my feet were on fire from wearing impractical but stunning shoes. Shopping for male sheep (rams or tups) to impregnate your ewes is a very, *very* different experience. Suffice to say I've grabbed more tits and nuts in my short farming career than your average GP.

What breed? What age? Is that a dip behind his shoulder? To begin with, the rule I lived by – much to Chris's dismay at times – was this: if a ram has a nice face and the swagger of a seventeen-year-old Gary Lucy (*Hollyoaks, Footballers' Wives*) wannabe who just got served a pint of Carlsberg with no ID, I was game.

But then I met Tyrone. He was a five-year-old pedigree blue Texel ram with the physique of a silverback gorilla, and our time together started at the local livestock market where I paid £150 for him. I'd gone with Chris and we looked round the different pens before breakfast. You remember which ones you like the look of, then watch out for them once the auction starts. I'd never actually bid for an animal before, but Tyrone had been surprisingly affectionate when I courageously put my hand through the bars to give him a stroke. That was what had made me like him.

The fact that he didn't butt my hand away should really have been a red flag: I've learned since then that friendly rams can be a huge no-no. They start thinking they're your boss, not the other way round, and it all ends in tears. But how was a rookie part-time farmer like me to know? I mentioned Tyrone to Chris – who hadn't seen him – and described him. 'You go and bid for him, then, babe,' he said. I don't think he thought I'd really do it. But when Tyrone strutted into the ring, I raised my hand, heart racing at a million miles an hour. A few minutes later, he was mine. What a buzz – I felt elated by the thrill of participating in a real live auction. Tyrone was my first independent purchase, and because of that, I loved him.

For the first few weeks, Tyrone was out with the ewes, which gave him plenty of opportunity to burn up his energy. But once all of them were covered – meaning pregnant – the boys were taken out and put together in a field. They're pretty fired up on testosterone at this point and can start to fight among themselves, backing away then charging aggressively, smashing their heads together and locking horns (if they have them). Rams sometimes weigh over a hundred kilos and more people die each year in attacks by rams than in attacks by bulls.

The first job we do in the mornings is called lookering: inspecting all our animals to make sure that everyone's on four feet, that no one's under the weather, and that all the water troughs are full. One day, I went into the rams' field and walked over to the trough to turn on the tap. To do that, I had to turn my back on the lads. That was when I heard the thump of hoofs – and whipped round to see Tyrone, head down, hurtling straight at me. Sheer instinct saved me: I yelled and waved my arms to scare him off, but I'd been on my own out there and I was pretty shaken. If he'd wanted to clatter me, he could have. And I knew it.

Later on, I mentioned what had happened to Chris, but I could see he thought I was being a bit dramatic about it. By then I'd also started to wonder: had Tyrone got confused? Had I made some mistake that might have triggered his behaviour? *I shouldn't have turned my back on him. That was it. Next time, I'll make sure I take more care.* But the moment I stepped back into his field, he charged at me again.

This time I rang Chris straight away, and I was crying.

I told him I was scared. He went up there to find out what was going on – and Tyrone charged at him too. Two weeks later, Tyrone was sent for slaughter. We didn't take the decision lightly, but we can't have volatile animals on the farm with public footpaths running through it – it's far too dangerous. I never should have bought him. I had to learn by my mistake.

Chris's new flock was growing steadily by now. As his circle of farming friends and contacts grew, he was also getting the chance to rent more land. We started grazing some rough hilly ground, which was part of a conservation scheme (the landowner is rewarded for taking care of it). The perfect sheep for that terrain, we found, were small-framed, slightly wild ewes, so we set about buying Shetlands, Soays, Herdwicks, Welsh Mountains and some other odds and sods.

It was while I was walking those hills that I started to think. There wasn't some big light-bulb moment where the path you should be taking is suddenly in front of you with a flashing neon sign reading *This Way*. In fact, at some point most days I was thinking, *What the fuck am I doing on a farm?* But I could learn to love this life, I thought – to really, truly love it. And I could feel myself getting hungry for it. I was also very much in love with Chris, and farming was his future. Nothing could have been clearer than that.

* * *

'Babe? There's been a lamb born up the hill.'

'Already?'

'Yeah.'

'But what about the snow?'

Chris hadn't been shepherding for long when the Beast from the East – a ferocious Siberian ice storm – came sweeping across the north of Europe. Ten inches of snow fell in one night, making many of the roads in Kent impassable, and in those terrible conditions it was difficult to get up the hill at all, so the landowner kindly started to do checks on the new flock. To make things even worse, Chris's autoimmune condition had just flared up and he was totally exhausted.

That premature lamb was in serious trouble – born far too soon in bitterly cold conditions that even a stronger full-term lamb might have struggled to survive. As Chris's stepdad drove him over there to check on it – he was feeling so rough that it wasn't safe for him to drive himself – he half expected he'd find the lamb frozen to death. I was miles away at home with the day off (no one could get into the salon for their appointments because of the atrocious weather), but he'd texted to tell me what was happening. The next thing that arrived was just a photo – but not at all the one I was expecting.

On my phone screen I saw Chris, taken by his stepdad, proudly holding his new lamb. Welsh Mountain sheep are 'hair sheep', with a thick coat round their shoulders almost like a lion's mane. With snowflakes piled on top of that, the mother looked majestic, like the monarch of some wild, wintry kingdom. I stood staring, totally amazed. Then the phone rang.

'Well – what do you think?' said Chris's voice.

'Oh, my God. That looks incredible. Boy or girl?'

'Girl. She's as wild as the hills. We've been chasing round trying to catch her in the snow drifts.'

Wow, I thought. The sheer resilience of that little thing was amazing. Plus – she was beautiful. Suddenly I felt a whole new future taking root in my mind. At first it was a very tiny seedling, but then it grew and grew. Maybe – just maybe – I should give farming a go.

* * *

Nature is exciting and sometimes filled with beauty – but it can also be harsh. The Beast from the East still had us tightly in its grip, which meant I was away from my job at the salon for days and could head out to the farm. Today I know how to dress for the weather but at that point I didn't have a clue: I'd gone on Amazon and bought myself and Chris these matching balaclavas. We put them on and drove through the snowstorm to the pregnant girls out on the Downs. Back then, we were hazy on details and biting our nails in case they all suddenly started delivering in the blizzard; that wouldn't happen now because we'd know exactly when they'd seen the ram and therefore the dates when their lambs were due. These ewes had also been bought with borrowed money – they were an investment by Chris in his farming future that he couldn't afford to repeat. All he could do to help them at this point was to get them in as tip-top physical condition as possible, so our plan was to feed them with sheep nuts (also known as 'ewe rolls'). These are packed with protein, vitamins and minerals to give the sheep the energy they need when they can't find any grass.

When we finally arrived and unloaded the sacks of sheep nuts from the truck, the weather was ferocious, with blasts of horizontal snow whipping right into our faces. I really wanted to impress Chris with my toughness and determination in these conditions, so although sheep nuts come in 25-kilo sacks, I hoisted one onto my shoulders and started staggering uphill. These days I'm physically far stronger and I've got my lifting techniques nailed, but back then it was almost too much for me. We stumbled out across the field calling to the ewes in very poor visibility. Once we'd found them – this didn't take long as they were pretty keen on the sheep-nuts idea – we took it in turns to tear slits in each other's bags then walked – stumbled – up and down so that the nuts made a trail behind us on the snowy ground. That way, the pregnant ewes would stand in a line to eat them rather than crowding around heaps of nuts and bashing into each other. Soon there was a row of happy bums as they all tucked in.

'Just cross your legs, girls. Cross your legs,' Chris told them urgently. 'You don't want to be lambing in this. It's too cold. Hold on till it's a little bit warmer.'

In the end, they did as he said, and only one or two delivered while there was still snow on the ground. But as soon as the bitter weather eased, the lambs really started coming: suddenly we had ten or more being born in a single day. We'd had a pretty narrow escape: no trailer yet, no barn yet, one of the team still very much part-time, and nothing to do but cross our fingers and keep praying, *Please no lambs, please no lambs*. Our system wasn't resilient – and if nature has one lesson, it's always to build in resilience. As absolute beginners back then, our only protection was good fortune – and we knew it.

* * *

'Babe? This can't be the one. It's just an empty field.'

'I sent you the Google Maps pin, Zo,' said Chris's patient voice, on my phone.

'I know – but, but, there's nobody here. Maybe you sent me the wrong pin.'

'Ping me your location.' I did. Apparently this was the place.

It was a damp, grey November day – real hair-frizzing weather – and I'd set out to change the battery on the electric fence in a new field Chris was renting and check that everybody there was on their feet. I'd overheard him taking phone calls about 'cover crops' and possible winter turnip grazing, but I wasn't exactly sure what that meant. I hadn't asked because I didn't want to sound clueless or expose myself (yet again) to the ditsy hair-dresser stereotype.

But this field was *definitely* empty. Deep, claggy mud and brown rocks stretched as far as the eye could see, and there were certainly no turnips. We'd have had the RSPCA on our backs pretty quickly if we left anyone to graze here anyway.

'There's no bloody sheep here!'

'Are you having a laugh?' Chris said to me. 'Rub your eyes and look again! Try to call them!'

'C'mon, girls, c'mon!' And then I heard a *beeeeh!* in the distance, and out from under the shelter of the trees, the sheep started heading my way.

That was when I realized that the 'rocks' I could see were actually the turnips. They're a root vegetable: the sheep eat the leaves, and once the turnips are left sitting on the soil – looking, to my untrained eyes, like stones – they eat those too, huge carby bulbs of goodness, a ban-quet fit for a king. I felt buzzing for those sheep – they looked so well, even if the air was hanging thick with the cabbage stench from their rear ends. What I'd mistaken for a patch of mud kept them fed for another week.

If a field is left unplanted and exposed, the soil wears away: that's erosion. Planting turnips, radishes and mus-tard is the solution. Once the field is a sea of green leaves, the woolly things move in, eat the crops and fertilize the ground. (Eat and poo, guys, eat and poo.) When they're done, there's no need to burn fossil fuels ploughing, and cereals can be planted straight away. It lets us feed our stock in winter and it helps the landowner too. This is just one of the ways in which farmers are tweaking how they work to secure the longevity of our food supply.

Never ever did I think I could be interested in anything like this. But here I was, among the turnips, learning how it all works. I was becoming more and more certain that this just might be my future – and a completely different one from anything I'd ever imagined. I could feel myself starting to evolve.

Then, suddenly, everything changed.

The Toughest Winter

I could hear my phone ringing in the bottom of my bag, but by the time I found it I had a missed call. It was Mum. Straight away I thought that was strange – she never normally calls me in the middle of the day.

I was on my lunch break at the salon, sitting in a coffee shop just around the corner. I phoned her back. 'Hey, Mum! You okay?'

Immediately I knew she wasn't. Her voice sounded really strained.

'I'm okay, yes, but this is going to come as rather a shock. It's Dad. You're going to have to come to the hospital.'

'Hospital! My God, Mum, why?'

'He's not well at all, I'm afraid.' Her voice cracked. 'It'll be easier to talk about it once you're here. Can you come, Zobes?'

'Of course!' I jumped up, rushed back to work and explained. My boss must have known from the expression on my face that it was serious. She was sweet and understanding and told me to go right away. 'Hospital', I knew without asking, would be the one in Maidstone nearest to my parents' home. The whole journey I grew more and more concerned.

I'd known in the back of my mind for quite a while that something wasn't right with Dad, but he was – well, he was *Dad*. I relied on him – we all did. He was always there, the man of the house for me, my mum, and my sister, Hollie, making us feel calm and secure. He never showed signs of weakness and was the backbone of our family. If I encountered any type of problem, there he was on speed-dial, like the time I lost my Oyster card and bank card and was stranded at Elephant and Castle tube station: he got the train up to rescue me. He once wired me my rent because I'd spent all my wages in Topshop (not proud of that). Solving the problem first, then discussing what I'd done wrong later was his style. On my first trip away with Chris, we went to a little shepherd's hut (ironic, I know) and the storm kettle didn't come with instructions. Within two minutes I was on the phone to Dad. Chris rolled his eyes and called me 'a princess'. But that was how it was: there was no problem too large or too small that Dad couldn't help with it, or at least advise me. I never considered that this situation could change.

For the last few months, he'd been suffering a fair amount with what the doctor diagnosed as sciatica – pain in his back that also travelled down his legs. He was seeing a chiropractor regularly and had a back support in the car for his hour-long commute to work each day, but other than that he was still seemingly well. Then one evening Hollie called me and said she'd just been round to Mum and Dad's. Dad had dropped a ton of weight, she told me – noticeably so. He had also been a bit aloof, which wasn't like him. This bothered me enough to ask Mum about it when I saw her and she mentioned that all the painkillers he was taking for his back were making him nauseous. They had also made him lose his sense of taste, she said, so he hadn't been eating. That sounded a bit weird but it made sense to me: I'd taken co-codamol, just the once, and it had made me feel as if I was going to throw up. Straight away, my phobia of sickness had kicked in hard. *Definitely no more co-codamol.* I could see why it might make Dad feel rough, so there was no cause for alarm.

Four weeks later, when I next saw him, he was off with me – off with everybody, really. He was either gravely worried about something he'd not mentioned, or the pain of his sciatica was getting to him. And I certainly agreed with Hollie about the weight loss – it was dramatic. His arms had folds of excess skin like you see on those body transformation shows on Channel 4. Looking back, I should have realized there was a serious problem with his health.

When I got to the hospital that day, it was clear pretty quickly just how bad this was. My grandpa, Tim, my auntie and Mum were there and when I asked exactly what was wrong, they started stuttering, stammering and beating around the bush. 'Just tell me what the fuck's going on!' I said to them.

Grandpa looked like he was going to have a coronary, hearing me swear, and Mum walked away crying. She couldn't face saying the words and watching my heart break. Dad was in a life-threatening condition, barely conscious with an oxygen mask over his face. His major organs were all shutting down. The doctors had zero explanations right now, but it was bad, really bad.

How on earth could he have been at work the day before and yet today he had lost the use of all his muscles and got himself stuck in the bath, resulting in being blue-lighted here? The doctors were thinking that it might be a superbug so all of us were wrapped up in full PPE.

'How long till Hollie gets here?' I asked Mum. My younger sister was at uni in Portsmouth.

'She's on her way now.'

When she arrived, I walked down to the ward entrance and met her so that she didn't have to take all this in by herself. She looked as shocked and disbelieving as I know

I must have done. The whole scene was like something out of *ER* – she probably thought she was hallucinating.

Dad was in intensive care for ten days. On day two, his CT scan showed up some 'shadows' – a term I found out very quickly was the medical code for cancer. The surgeon then did biopsies to find out exactly what the shadows were, but Dad was on a ward before we had the results. That was when the nightmare got a hundred times worse. His crippling sciatica? Bone cancer. His forgetfulness? Curiously, that was caused by liver cancer. And he had a little adrenal-gland cancer thrown in for good measure. Doctors don't offer predictions of how long someone will live, but we asked the question. Later we found that Dad had asked it too, but he never told us – even then, he was still trying to protect us. The doctors said that the best case/kindest scenario would be if a blood clot travelled to his heart: an embolism, which would bring his life to a close. We listened, trying to take all this in, but it just felt completely unreal.

No one could say exactly how long Dad would live, but it was clear that the time left was measured in weeks. It turned out to be five. In the face of a real, world-rocking crisis, people often rise to the occasion. That was certainly true of my family, and I hope it was also true of me. You'd think that the entire period would have been a blur of confusion, but that's not what happened. Instead of feeling bewildered and lost, I became alert and observant, soaking in every detail of what happened while experiencing immense sadness. Loss, or in this case impending loss, is like a physical pain, and the feelings come in waves. I could barely eat, but we survived on Starbars, easy-peel satsumas, posh mango yuzu yoghurts and Ribena Light. Whenever I got a tiny pang of hunger and thought I should have something a bit more substantial to keep my strength up, I'd grab a curly-edged canteen sandwich. But after just one mouthful, another wave of grief would start to rise. I'd feel as though my insides were being incinerated and quickly ditch the sarnie.

My mum, Hollie and I got into a groove when Dad was still in the hospital, taking it in turns to spend sleepless nights on a fold-up camp bed alongside him, giving him leg and foot massages and bringing mocha coffees, which he kept asking for but never seemed to drink. His taste buds never worked properly again and it was hard to know what he'd eat, and also tricky to get him to drink enough; the nurses kept telling us he was getting dehydrated. One afternoon he said he fancied something spicy so I rustled up a chilli con carne and brought it along in a plastic container, but the second he tasted it, he started fanning his mouth and gasping for air. I tried to stay calm, thinking I'd overdone it with the spice, but then he grabbed his Ribena and downed the entire bottle. The nurses were delighted that at least we'd solved the dehydration problem. All any of us could do, we decided, was to try our best.

We didn't want Dad to die in a hospital, so we decided

to bring him home. There wasn't enough time to organize a care team, so Mum, Hollie and I decided we would handle his round-the-clock care. We had a quick rethink of the house and installed two beds in the dining room. Dad's pride and determination meant he wanted to walk in rather than being wheeled in a chair, and he managed it – what an entrance! My insides were in a state of pure elation and celebratory tears were flowing. We had posh fish goujons from the deli counter for tea that night, although Dad added some very weird sauces. It was quite comical how the cancer had altered his eating habits. He went for really strange combinations of flavours now and when Hollie made proper focaccia – it took her hours on a scorching day – he drowned the whole thing in piccalilli. She might as well not have bothered.

Dad was on a lot of drugs, including morphine, and the nurses warned us this might make him confused as time went on. There were so many tablets that I'm surprised he didn't rattle when he moved, and we drew up a chart so that Mum, Hollie and I, plus the three nurses who visited regularly, could track which ones he'd taken. It was a huge responsibility – the most I'd ever had: on each shift it was down to me to get Dad's doses right, the timings and all of his care. It felt daunting, but it's amazing what you can take in your stride when you have no choice. We just rolled up our sleeves, put on our big-girl pants and got on with it. It was also an honour: he had looked after us for so long and now we could look after him. I felt good about that, not to mention being over the moon that he remembered my name and who I was right to the end.

Work on the farm had also made me physically stronger than I'd ever been before. One afternoon when Dad needed a wee but struggled to get up, I was standing on the bed behind him. Hollie and Mum were in front, trying to negotiate with him about how we were going to help him move. We were pretty worn out and the situation was a bit overwhelming. All of us were close to tears. I suddenly realized what the problem was: Dad didn't know my strength from all the farm work I was doing so he thought I couldn't manage his weight. It must be hard sometimes for parents to recognize when their children have grown up, and he was so ill by now that there was no way to explain how much I'd changed without confusing him. The most important thing was that he felt loved.

Deep down, I'd always believed I was a vulnerable, sensitive soul, in tears at the drop of a hat: an *EastEnders'* plot line or a sad story from one of my clients was more than enough to set me off. So the strength on every level – emotional and physical – that I found during those weeks of Dad's illness seemed to come from nowhere. Perhaps it was from a place inside me, a deep self I'd not been aware of until now. The most important thing I learned is that crying is not a sign of weakness, it's a sign of feeling. I became very conscious of this.

Overnight, surreal situations became the norm. Did

I ever think I'd be putting lip balm on my terminally ill father's chapped lips? No. Did I ever think I'd be dunking his inert hand in a washing-up bowl of clay to make a cast? Definitely not. The idea of making moulds of our hands linked with his came from Hollie's Pinterest board – and what a palaver it turned out to be. Five shops and £150 later, we had the materials we needed and we set about trying to make our own version of this sentimental masterpiece. There was a point during the ten minutes when I was holding Dad's hand in the bucket of goo that I started getting hot and prickly at the thought of how we would explain what we were doing to his nurse if one turned up. But the results were surprisingly good, considering we could barely talk through all our giggling. Dad had flakes of white clay under his nails until his dying day.

We'd been just about living at the hospital for two weeks, and then once Dad was home we spent all our time with him. I'd barely seen Chris for the last month. He was sending messages and phoning me. I knew he understood what I was going through because he had lost his dad. But one day he rang me. 'You and Hollie – you need to take a breather,' he said firmly, and he came round in the van to pick us up. We felt nervous and weird to be leaving, but Mum agreed with Chris – she could manage and she thought it would be good for us.

Chris drove us up onto the Downs. The last time I'd been there, only a few lambs had been born. Now they were everywhere. Hollie, Chris and I stood together in the big green stillness, all of us breathing very slowly, soaking up the peace. As I listened to the bleating of the ewes and their lambs answering, I realized Chris had known what I needed before I did. We couldn't be together much in the chaos going on, but our relationship was growing stronger. And then – unbelievably enough – a lamb was born right there, the first that Hollie ever saw. I took a photo of her with it. She told me afterwards what that moment was like for her: at a time when nothing seemed quite real, it was almost an out-of-body experience, she said. With dying, grieving and loss all around, new life seemed like a little miracle.

'We'll have to get back now,' I said to Chris.

'Sure, Zo.' He reached into his pocket for his keys. And then his other pocket. And then the back pockets of his jeans. He looked aghast.

'Everything okay, babe?' I asked him.

'Um . . . I think I dropped my keys.'

'Where were you standing when you last had them?'

'Dunno. They're round here somewhere.'

We all dropped to our knees and started crawling about trying to find them. Hollie and I didn't say anything because neither of us wanted to make him feel guilty, but we were really freaking out. This was a *terrible* time to get stranded on the Downs, with Mum on her own back at the house. What if we couldn't find them? After a few minutes of us suppressing our panic and frantically patting the ground, Chris started texting a friend to ask if he could come and get us. Then Hollie said suddenly, 'Hey – got them!' and disaster was averted. In this crazy parallel universe of illness and grief, it was strange to find out that normal stuff still happened – like losing the car keys.

I tried to discover what dying was like, what to expect and the signs that it's near. But I couldn't find the answers, no matter how many internet forums I trawled in the early hours. I also started talking to Dad, telling him my deepest darkest secrets and even coming clean about some rather larger boy-related fibs from my teens. I wanted him to feel that our relationship was one of total peace and trust now – that I was fine, a grown-up woman and he had done a great job. Although I didn't want to let him go, he didn't have to hang around and suffer just to be there for me.

By now it was almost five weeks since he had become ill and it was clear that he didn't have much longer. We hoped he might drift off peacefully in his sleep, but that wasn't quite how it was. I've got nothing to compare with what actually happened when he died but I'd say that his passing, when it came, was pretty close to perfect. I wouldn't class his death as peaceful, but at least we were all together at the home Hollie and I were raised in and I'm incredibly thankful for that. As he grew weaker and weaker, he started Cheyne-Stokes breathing, which is what people call the 'death rattle' because it often occurs when death is close and someone's heart is starting to fail. One night, there was the most tremendous thunderstorm, and as I watched it out of the window and looked at him lying there, I thought, *Right, this is it – he's going out with a bang.* But – nope.

I had watched him through the night so in the morning I went to take a nap while Hollie took over. But a little while later she woke me and told me she thought it really was time. Dad was deeply unconscious by now and we all sat around him on the bed, watching him trying to catch each loud, phlegmy breath, all on tenterhooks as to whether there would be another or if this was the finale. We didn't want those breaths to stop, but the struggle to keep going seemed so brutal. I laid my hand on his chest and felt his heartbeat. It started getting out of rhythm and I realized this was it. As he passed, he opened his eyes wide and looked straight at the photo of the four of us that we'd put at the side of his bed. And then I felt his heart stop – a surreal moment, but not unwelcome. And that was the end. I didn't see his spirit leave his body or anything. I do feel I'm open to that kind of experience, so I'd been wondering if I would.

Nobody had warned me about how quickly a body loses its warmth after death or how the skin drains of colour, like a zombie in a horror film. After a couple of minutes, Dad was even less recognizable. I wasn't expecting that, and it took my breath away. I wish I'd been forewarned about those natural changes – it would have helped me to feel more prepared. I'd envisaged sitting with him afterwards, taking the time to say goodbye, but I didn't want the last image I had of him to be scary, so I decided to step outside.

Still, that evening at home was very calm. His body had been taken away by the funeral director. Mum, Hollie and I had been living in each other's pockets for weeks in a high-tension, high-stress environment, and Dad's death allowed us to take our own space for a while and to give space to each other. I had a bath and Mum sat for a while by herself at the end of the garden. But then we came together again and chatted, all three of us wearing Dad's T-shirts as nighties. There was an air of quiet comfort, even relief – a bit like when you've been on holiday and now it's your first night home in fresh pyjamas, eating snacks you couldn't get abroad. I guess we'd been away from normal life for nearly six weeks.

The three of us had one last thing to discuss: Dad's 'send-off'. We were all very much on the same page about this: no gleaming polished box, no stuffy crematorium. His childhood had been spent outside in the fresh air with his collies, camping, building rope swings, and then he'd become a rebellious teen, getting expelled from a posh boys' grammar school.

He had gone straight to work as a sound technician and one of his first gigs was working on the Live Aid show at Wembley in the summer of 1985, getting photographs of Freddie Mercury and Adam Ant, among others. He went on tour around the globe with some of the world's most influential bands and was even involved in the then Prince of Wales's fiftieth birthday bash. But he'd taken it all in his stride and I wouldn't be surprised if he never fangirled once in his entire career – the very definition of cool in my eyes.

His thirty-odd years' rubbing shoulders with pop stars and celebs meant that Dad didn't care about glitz and glamour – quite the opposite: he was a simple man with simple tastes. We ended up with a celebratory festival: we spent three days lovingly decorating his coffin with photographs and paintings, then propped it on hay bales in the marquee we'd rented, surrounded it with wildflowers and held a barbecue. There was a top-of-the-range sound system too, obviously. We all got dolled up in bright colours and patterns, and people were arriving from all over the country – his old work colleagues from the eighties, friends from school and close family friends. Mum had asked me if I wanted to say something: I definitely did and I planned it quite carefully – but when I stood up I changed my mind and didn't follow my notes. I found I could speak without having to think too much about what I was saying. I even made some jokes.

Standing next to Dad's hand-painted coffin in my bright yellow dress was the only surreal bit. It seemed impossible that he could be inside. It was also a bloody hot day and my farming experience had given me an understanding that dead sheep start to decompose really quickly. What did it smell like in that box? What did he look like now? They aren't the greatest thoughts to have racing through your mind – but that's what grief is like: it takes you right to the nub of things. You've no energy to avoid the harsh realities. I just hoped they'd remembered to put his hat in there with him.

A hearse collected his body in the early evening and we lined the field to toast him with cider and champagne as he went on his way. He would have absolutely hated the attention. And then we danced late into the evening. Weirdly, it was one of the best days of my life. We had managed to pull off what we'd set out to do and it had been spectacular.

But there's no way to get around grief. The hardest part of loss is what comes after: the time when you're supposed to move on. The absence of the person you love is the new normal and you have to get on with it. Except you're paralysed with pain. Something else as well – *it doesn't feel final at the time.* I'm no psychiatrist so I can't tell you the scientific reason why, but perhaps a part of us is too optimistic to accept what's happened. You don't want to never, never *ever* see or speak again to the person you love. And somehow some tiny irrational bit of hope stays alive inside you – that if you try hard enough, you'll find your way back to them. You'll hold one last conversation. You'll hug them one more time.

But death is the end. You can speak to them in your head. You may believe their spirit comes back to visit you sometimes on Earth. You can play their favourite music and eat their favourite meals. Those things can help you to feel closer, but ultimately the person is gone. For me, that's the hardest lesson of them all. I can't just pick up the phone and ask Dad how to change my brake light. I can't roll my eyes that he still insists on hugging me goodnight even when I'm twenty-five and give him my cheek really quickly because it's not 'cool' to kiss your dad goodbye before getting on a train. I can't even be mad when he locks the car windows and lets out a huge fart as he silently giggles. Because he doesn't fart any more. He doesn't kiss or hug me any more.

I envy the Vikings, not just for their stunning braids and hunky men but for their beliefs. They didn't fear death because they would be seeing each other in Valhalla. I'm choosing the Vikings as an example because they fascinate me, but many faiths have beliefs about life after death and even reincarnation. I understand why those views bring comfort, but they don't work for me. I see Dad in my dreams but I don't believe I'll ever actually see him again. And that's the work of grieving – learning to live alongside your loss, not be in so much pain that you can't function, and eventually to find happiness once more. But that process is brutally hard. And while I was struggling to get my head around losing Dad, yet another catastrophe struck us.

I was heartbroken when Dad died because he would never be a grandpa. But he'd lived to the fullest while he could. That's all any of us can hope for, isn't it? And that meant I could find acceptance – which was the complete opposite to my mood after Jimmy's death six months later. With Dad we had known, for a little while at least, what was coming.

Jimmy had been Chris's best friend and partner in crime when we were growing up. I'd known him a little back then, a skinny kid with a long fringe who walked with his head on a slant and wore black jeans and hoodies even in blistering heat. He and Chris grew up together, riding mopeds into the early hours, listening to the Streets, and of course there was the time they discovered Jimmy couldn't swim – once he was in the lake. (Along with all sorts of other mischief I daren't even ask about.) The two of them still lived around the corner from each other and years later, when Chris and I were dating and Chris started to be seriously unwell, he'd often go and lie on Jimmy's mum's sofa for a chat. He loved that sense of normality and friendship, and I started going round there with him. We'd take Indie with us, and Jimmy adored her, playing and throwing toys for her long after Chris and I had given up. I can count on one hand the list of people we would feel comfortable leaving her with if a problem were ever to arise – she's an oddball who needs lots of love and understanding. Jimmy was so gentle and quiet that he never made her feel frightened or threatened.

Unbeknown to us, he'd been ill for a while, but his death still came as a shock. It was very sudden and he didn't suffer, but it happened while he was on his own. He'd phoned into work sick the day before he died, then in the morning when he didn't call again, his colleagues wondered where he was and tried ringing him. No answer. Still no answer hours later. More and more concern – and eventually Jimmy's sister and Chris went round to his house. Chris had to climb in through a window, and he found his friend's body.

Jimmy's death was one of those tragedies that shapes your future. It left a trail of guilt and unhappiness behind in a way my dad's death hadn't. First there was the shock. There'd been no warning and he'd had no chance to tie up any loose ends. Everyone felt awful that he'd died on his own, even though none of us could have known. Until the medical investigations were complete, there wasn't even a reason why. I remember talking with his sister and hearing her words flowing out of her, like lava escaping a volcano. I realized then how badly they would burn her if she kept them inside.

Pain was all around. In my mum's house, all we could feel every second was that Dad wasn't there. And now my closest friends were broken by yet another loss: every time we all met up, Jimmy wasn't there. Dad's funeral day had been full of sunshine, but by now it was late autumn. We were plunged into the bleak darkness of winter.

Grief. That word isn't nearly huge enough to capture the myriad experiences contained within the process. Grief can mean getting yourself dolled up, incredibly overdressed, for a trip to the post office, just to make sure you keep up the impression that you're 'coping'. At the next minute, grief can mean worrying that because you look fine, which of course you'd intended to do, everyone will assume that you *are* fine so nobody will help you. (If that sounds confusing, it captures the feeling!) Grief can mean taking on a dead person's catchphrases as your own to keep them alive, or wearing their clothes. Grief can mean not washing and residing in an unhygienic pit of mess, eating nothing but satsumas because that's all you can stomach.

Grief is the pain that comes over you at the smallest and most ridiculous things, like when I needed a tool to punch a new hole in my belt and knew it was exactly the type of thing my dad would have had stashed away somewhere. Or when I realized I'd just folded a sheet of kitchen roll perfectly to use as a coaster and that I'd watched him do that exact thing hundreds of times. Grief means opening your eyes at 2 a.m. from a dream in which that person seemed so real you have tears cascading down your cheeks; you try with all of your might to fall back to sleep, to re-enter that dream for ten more seconds to soak up the image of them because you don't know when you'll get the next chance.

The only thing I'm certain of is that you can gauge your grief on how much you loved that person. So it's really a privilege, an emotion you've received due to the love you were able to feel. When you think of it that way, it does put a small positive spin on it. Grief is a whirl-wind so don't try to control it – just feel it. The ability to grieve is a blessing.

* * *

I grasped pretty quickly that going back to the salon wasn't an option. My world had been turned upside down and I no longer had it in me to be sympathetic when my client was having a meltdown over little Archie spilling his Frube on her Range Rover seats. Those clients were entitled to the best service I could give – it's what they were choosing to pay for. So how could I provide them with less than before? If my heart wasn't in it any more, it was time to get out.

On the farm, life carried on. Nothing had changed: the hay racks needed filling and the water trough in the back field was still broken. The animals treated me just the same. Chris and I never had one big conversation when he said, 'Hey, babe, come and be a farmer.' It happened gradually, with me testing the waters, dropping in the odd comment about how it might work for me and him thinking, *Yeah, maybe . . .*

It wasn't until later that he told me what was going through his mind. He could see I loved lambing, but that was springtime. Was I really cut out for farming winters? Okay, I'd seen one snowstorm, but the long cold months are remorseless and rough. How would I manage then?

But here's where Chris and I are most alike: we can be impulsive. Looking back, I realize that both of us took this epic, life-changing decision on an impulse. Our decision was *Hell, yeah – so why not?*

There's so much encouragement to 'be kind to yourself' when you're going through a tough time that it almost starts to put you under pressure. It goes hand in hand with the look people give you when they see you for the first time after a tragedy – the head tilt, the slightly upturned mouth and the well-meaning speech about 'Remember to take all the time you need.' But take the time to do what? There isn't a foolproof guide we must follow. And there are no rights and wrongs: just whatever you need to get you through the next hour, the next day, the big anniversaries or 'firsts' since you experienced your loss. Perhaps some of those coping mechanisms won't be the healthiest, but this is about surviving, about keeping on breathing any way you can. I've learned since then that some bereaved people spend years hopping from project to project, filling in the gaps with activities so that their sense of loss can't creep in too strongly or deeply, terrified they'll spiral out of control.

For me, the coping mechanism turned out to be calf-rearing. I'd worked my fortnight's notice at the salon, and suddenly there I was: full-time. Chris remembered how I loved nursing Fred and George, the first two 'die-ers' he ever bought me, so as we headed into winter, the quietest period of the year, he decided to give me a section of the rented farm that was mine: a stake in our new life together. The farm was about twenty minutes' drive from our house so it would carve out a routine for me, and act as a learning curve. I'm also sure he knew that it would help me with my grief and give me a chance to gain confidence. Anyway, I was in so much death-induced pain that I had to do something, so he surprised me on my wet, cold and miserable birthday that October with a new (second-hand) milk bar for calf-feeding – undoubtedly my best present ever.

The build-up to bringing the calves home to the farm was intense: building the pens in the shed; educating myself on calf nutrition, vaccinations, biology, common practices. When the animals arrived, they turned out to be a lot of work, but I threw myself into it head-first, skipping meals, working myself to the bone. The grief and hurt that were pouring through my veins had to be soothed by something, and for me it was those calves. With their incessant mooing, I could no longer hear myself think, and the inner silence washed over me, like a massive wave of relief. A friend once told me that wild swimming has the same effect, but I'm not willing to risk catching dysentery from the Thames or end up picking used hypodermic needles out of my feet. So here we are – calf rearer of the year!

I had found something to do that made me feel love, so I did it till I'd nothing left to give. Those new pens were where I could let myself go and take down my barriers.

I could be as raw and hurt as I wanted, with no one watching. I learned so much from those hours alone in that barn. I cried a lot of tears feeding the calves, which sounds so depressing but wasn't at all. It was just me grieving in the purest of ways. The animals didn't judge me for the snot running down my face into my mouth or for playing the Streets' album *Original Pirate Material* over and over again. Being with them became my therapy. The routines of caring for them gave me space to breathe. I'd needed to find a route through grief, and the calves provided it.

My friends seemed to be moving on in life: getting a foot on the first precarious rung of the property ladder, doing the sensible stuff that I'd always expected I would do. They might have the two-up-two-down to call their own, but could they heal their broken hearts by deciding to submerge themselves in calf rearing? Well, okay, technically yes – but it was highly unlikely to happen. I loved doing this – I truly, deeply loved it. And I found it gave me something more important than those sensible things ever could.

Grieving for Dad had changed me. I think it gave me faith. Faith in myself that nature would help me mend, along with the confidence that anything thrown at me couldn't rival what I'd already been through. Whatever happened next, I knew I could survive.

* * *

I only lost one calf in the first year I reared them, a seemingly healthy female that went from fine to dead in five hours. Losing lambs is upsetting, but somehow a dead calf was different. Perhaps it's because they have more personality, or maybe it's the size and weight of the body that makes them feel so present. A dead sheep or lamb goes in the dead bin (which is a red wheelie bin) that you get from the fallen-stock man, who is also known as the 'deadman'. He comes round with a truck to empty it – it's not pleasant, but it's fairly straightforward. During the winter when we lose more animals in harsher conditions, or during lambing when there are always losses, we can call whenever the bin needs to be emptied.

With a calf, it's different. They're too heavy to lift into the bin, so they have to be collected and removed. A clamp needs to be attached to its leg and it's then hoisted into the back of the van. I was unprepared for a huge dead calf leaving a trail of snot along the yard: when an animal (or human for that matter) dies, fluid comes out of the body. The guys in the van seemed to take it in their stride and went on chatting about the weather (and what was the alternative? To get a team of bearers round to carry the calf onto the truck while singing 'Wind Beneath My Wings'?). Still, it left me feeling very shaken.

Choosing to work in one of the country's most demanding and intense industries while suffering blinding grief might sound like a breakdown waiting to happen – and you wouldn't be wrong about that: as a farmer you're affected by every single life lost. Picking up lifeless lambs from the field, cold and stiff as a board, or the stench of the 'dead bin' in summer – none of it is easy. But it's part of the job. You soon learn that if you dwell on death, you won't survive as a farmer. You have to focus on life.

As spring arrived at last, lambing became a real comfort. I felt at home when we were in the thick of it, a sense of belonging. Saving lives and nurturing all the orphan lambs brought a sense of usefulness and meaning. I'd been longing for that feeling. The living world around me had got me through my toughest winter.

And Now We're Farming!

'Okay . . . Pull her onto her arse so she doesn't kick you!'

Grunting with effort, I heaved the sheep into a sitting position on her bum, leaning against my legs. 'Like this?'

'Yep,' Chris said. 'Now bend her head back and down. That'll stop her thrashing.'

Finally, I had her in position. From the smell of her hoofs, I didn't have to ask which side had foot-rot. The stench was awful, a bit like the food-waste bin before you have to bleach it.

'See that white chalky bit of hoof, Zo? That's the bit that needs to come off.'

I picked up the clippers. A ewe's foot has a soft fleshy

bit between the toes, then two hoof sections, which have to be flat so she can walk. One was overgrown, allowing bacteria to get down into her hoof, and now there was an infection.

'So now I trim it down?' I asked.

'Go ahead. Like tha— *No! Woah!* Not that deep or it'll be pissing out blood!'

'Right,' I muttered. I couldn't help wondering what had happened to my scissor skills since I'd left the salon. My second attempt was much better, and now at least Chris was looking pleased. A bit of antiseptic spray and the ewe was good to go.

'How did that feel, darlin'?' I asked the ewe, as she wriggled away. 'Your first pedicure in Zoë's salon!'

Quitting my job as a hairdresser to be a full-time farmer was one of the scariest things I've ever done. No guaranteed income. No guaranteed happiness. But then, I don't have a guaranteed lifespan either. That had been made very clear to me during the year I'd just endured. So I bought some waterproofs . . . *and now we're farming!* Those four words became a joke that Chris and I made to each other – still do, to this day – but they were deadly serious too. There was no going back.

It was a massive challenge. For a start, I was going to be glued to my boyfriend's side for twenty-four hours every day – something that might strain even the strongest relationship. And as if that wasn't enough, he would have to teach me – from scratch – a way of life that he'd had in his blood from his earliest days. I've described already how Chris's dad's death when he was twelve led to his family giving up farming. The loss of a parent and the only home he'd known created havoc in his young life and meant he understood what I was going through after my dad died. I found this immensely comforting. But he also had farming experience in his memory banks from the years he'd lived with animals and cared for them. He could rely on the skills he'd inherited from his father and grandfather. He would *never* understand what it was to be a farming novice. He's instinctive. I'm not. And it shows.

As for me – I'd had a life plan in place since I was twelve. There was zero wiggle room: find a man, fall in love, buy a house, buy a dog, get engaged, married, pregnant, babies times three, live happily ever after, the end. Looking back, I can see that I'd made no allowance for real life, and I think that was my biggest mistake. This seemingly harmless plan was very limiting. It had dictated who I was, and who I allowed myself to be, for more time than I care to remember.

On top of that, watching *The Hills* and *Footballers' Wives* had exacerbated my unrealistic longing for glamorous love with all the trimmings (and also for French manicures and heavy side fringes). When I was a child, I would Tipp-Ex the tips of my grubby prepubescent nails to get The Look – because Tipp-Ex is the same as a French manicure, right? – then put a cheap ring from Claire's Accessories on my engagement finger before popping over to Safeway with Mum. I became obsessed with being in love. I prayed that Ron Weasley and Hermione Granger from Harry Potter would hook up and – years later – I grieved a break-up with my first boyfriend by sobbing into my pillow, listening to The Libertines and eating Häagen-Dazs. I can't believe now how many nights I spent dreaming of waking up to a text expressing that lad's undying passion for me and my beauty, then of him turning up unannounced on my shabby South London doorstep with fresh pastel de natas from my favourite bakery, just like in the films.

As I grew up, I got more in touch with who I really am and real-life experience taught me a few home truths. The sickly sweet ideology of love is make-believe: it belongs in books and films and on the pages of glossy magazines . . . and, these days, on the phone screen as well (thank you, social media). It shouldn't be a life goal – it's far too arbitrary.

But that chocolate-box life plan of mine had stayed basically in place. I was hoping that a relationship with a boy would, at some point, turn into a keeper and then there'd be a wedding – lots of fishtail dress fantasies going on here, with all my closest friends as Team Bride, having a wonderful time at the hen do with as much willy-related memorabilia as possible. (And there would *definitely* be a male stripper.) After that, of course, we'd buy a house. Then there'd be our babies and a happy-ever-after.

But now we'd gone rogue. We were completely off-piste

with that life plan. For me as a full-time farmer, every-thing had changed – and my future looked very differ-ent too. While I was excited, the strategist in me was screaming, 'SOS!' *So what happens now? What next? What about the Plan?* If I could change one thing about those early days, it would be this: I wish I'd found it easier to go with the flow a little more. Instead, I was constantly looking ahead and worrying. It was hard to shut the lid on my perfect chocolate-box life. In some ways, it's still a work in progress.

* * *

I didn't make a grand announcement in the salon: *I'm leaving to go and be a farmer!* I'd been off work for more than seven weeks while Dad was dying, and afterwards I went back only to complete my fortnight's notice. That gave me a chance to say goodbye to some of my clients, and to tell them what I was going to do next. Quite a few were struggling to imagine my new life and that was where the idea for my 'Chief Shepherdess' Instagram account came in: I started it so they could see, first, that I hadn't invented the whole thing, and second, to show them what on earth we were up to.

Mum was surprisingly cool with it. There was no doubt in her mind that this was what I needed to do. 'To be honest, Zobes,' she said, 'your dad and I both knew that if you were going to do something it was what you were going to do and there was no way to stop you.' She had that right. There wasn't even one big moving day. Before my dad was sick, I'd been staying at Chris's house more and more. I gradually just stopped going home, and started doing the washing for both of us.

Chris was expanding his rented farmland. Now that I was on board, we could work on it together. We had little business cards printed up that read: *Do you need sheep to graze this land?* When we saw an empty field, we'd leave our cards on the fence. He'd already sold his Transit and bought a pick-up truck, and now it was my turn: I sold my little Corsa and bought a 4x4 because I'd be needing a four-wheel drive for going off-road. And if I had to fit a sheep into the back, now I could. My trainers became (posh) wellies (more than one pair needed now) and all my clothes were for farming. My hair had 'farmer highlights', consisting mostly of rogue bits of hay stuck in my fringe. My internet search history read 'What is listeria?' and 'How old is a hogget?' instead of 'Can you die from a hangover?' Then Chris's dad's mate Ian gave us a trailer so that we could move our animals about. Once we'd given it a bit of TLC and started towing it, we really felt like farmers.

Another lifestyle change was with our friends. Up to now, Chris had had his and I'd had mine. That was fine, but now we began to have farming friendships together. Instead of popping out for brunch or going on a drinking night, we might all go to a sheep sale, or to see vintage tractors. We were living with his mum and stepdad, which I'd have been mortified to admit even when I was twenty, let alone in sight of thirty – but it was all about priorities now. We chose to make a life for ourselves on the farm: to have that lifestyle – and all the stories we'd have to tell – rather than cars with heated steering wheels and buying a house together. I'm at peace with our decision (mostly).

I also had a huge amount to learn, but to start with it was hard to ask the really basic questions – things that a farmer from birth wouldn't even have to think about, but which would never have crossed a hairdresser's mind. What happens, for example, when a dead animal is removed from a farm? I knew they couldn't enter the food chain because nothing can unless it's been killed at a certified abattoir – so where do they go? (It's astounding when you dig deep into the process of disposal. Some go into plastics and latex. Some end up in your make-up.)

Every detail about farming fascinated me. My ears were constantly pricked and I suddenly found I had skills in retaining information that I wish had been available to me at school. Better late than never, I suppose. It just goes to show how vital it is that children's lessons are made interesting and relevant. It's when you really love something that the knowledge sticks – just like the lyrics of TLC's song 'No Scrubs' from when I was a child, which are engraved on my brain.

So, now it wasn't the latest gossip on Buzzfeed that got me hot under the collar. It was finding out that sheep don't have top teeth at the front, and there is such a thing as 'red diesel' that's prohibited in road vehicles. I filled a series of dog-eared notebooks with tricks I'd learned, plus tried-and-tested methods I'd picked up over the few months I had lived as a livestock carer. Who knows – maybe somebody needs them? Perhaps there's a gap in the market for *Livestock For Dummies*.

We always say how fortunate Chris was that I was interested in learning to work with the animals. If I hadn't been, what would have happened? Would I have become second to his work? Would he pretend to enjoy a Sunday stroll round Covent Garden in clean shoes when he'd rather be fixing the fencing over the back orchard to stop the rams getting in with the ewes? Would the overpriced Starbucks – his only consolation – be enough? Could that have worked for us? Maybe, for a while. But not for long.

* * *

'Bloody hell, Zo – those are looking well!'

The pet pen was mine – all my own work – and its occupants were thriving. Right from the start, it was where I really felt in charge. Chris didn't have the patience to sit with the orphan lambs and feed them but I enjoyed it: I'd take along the feeding bucket with its six teats and use it as my chance to draw a breath in all the non-stop action and high-intensity learning I was involved in. When one of Chris's friends – a very experienced farmer – came round fox-shooting for us to keep the number of preda-tors down and protect our flock, he saw the pen and thought I was doing a great job. It really was the biggest compliment he could have paid me.

On the first evening I went out to see my friends, I left Chris an A4 sheet of instructions for the pen: who to latch on first, because if you don't they'll miss out, who needs unlatching because otherwise they'll overeat. (You can tell when a lamb's belly is full, and ewes will push a lamb off the teat once they know it's had enough.) I texted Chris later and he told me everything was fine . . . then mentioned briefly that he wasn't sure how much some of them were meant to have and that some were drinking much faster than the others. That was when I began to have concerns.

Next morning when I went into the pen, I could see straight away we were in trouble. Two of the lambs had tummies like beach balls, round and rock solid. So much for my instruction sheet – Chris must have *really* let them guzzle the evening before. As gas builds up in a lamb's little stomach, it puts pressure on its organs and can even crush its lungs. It's called bloat and animals can die, so when it happens, you don't have long to deal with it.

I manoeuvred a soft tube into the side of the first lamb's mouth and down its throat into its belly so that I could dose it with vegetable oil to neutralize the gas. Then I repeated the process with the second. By the time the next feed came around, there was a good chance that they'd both be okay. But four hours later, only one was. The second still looked swollen and miserable, hanging back away from the group, hunched over with its back rounded, and kicking its legs, a sure sign of stomach cramps. I could see its laboured breathing as its distended stomach pressed against its diaphragm.

I needed to do something to release the pressure. On the farm we have many different sizes of needles and syringes, and I'd noticed lots of Instagram posts about solving this problem. But doing the procedure on my own for the first time was scary. I grabbed my phone, brought up YouTube, which has dozens of 'treat your bloated lamb' videos, and watched a quick refresher from a young US farmer with a super laid-back manner as he went through what to do. I was shaking like a leaf but I did what he said and popped a needle through the lamb's skin at the side of its abdomen to relieve the pressure. It worked. The lamb improved quickly and I was really chuffed. I wore my new vet hat that day, and a superhero cloak for good measure.

It can help to think outside the box sometimes as the animals can't tell us where it hurts. When we're dealing with illness, we try everything we can – hippy-dippy treatment or not – before we give antibiotics or strong medication, but of course if they're in pain or at death's door, we go straight for the conventional treatments. It amazes me how quickly I've been able to pick up that intuition about our animals. As soon as I enter the barn nowadays, I can tell you if someone is feeling off colour. Being vigilant saves lives, along with my steadily growing veterinary knowledge.

Whenever we went to the livestock market in those early days, I stuck very close to Chris. If he went to the loo, I'd head out to the café rather than stay there on my own. But as I grew in confidence, he started to leave me ringside without either of us really thinking about it. Okay, so I was still the only one there not wearing a flat cap or a beanie with the name of an agricultural feed company on it, but I was starting to feel part of the industry.

* * *

Raise your hand if you were under the impression farmers are rich. Same, babe, same. They drive shiny Land Rovers and live in huge country houses with Agas and utility rooms with heated stone floors. They wear floor-length waxed jackets teamed with that welly brand – Le Chameau – my common self can never pronounce. (Everybody in the business just calls them 'shammies'.)

I can now confirm with a fair amount of certainty that all the above statements are largely false, though to start with I was pretty surprised by the gap between perception and reality. A farmer's financial turnover may look reasonably healthy from a distance, but if you break it down to an hourly wage, well, I can't even hazard a guess, but I soon grasped that I could earn more money sewing gussets on polyester knickers in a dingy basement somewhere. The truth is: most of us don't do this for the money or for the plush lifestyle. If we did, we'd be pretty disappointed because we don't have either.

In most industries, I've noticed that the top dogs get the bling – the £100K cars, the sparkly watches, the vintage Chanel sunnies. The successful people tend to stand out. But that's not quite so true within the farming community, or not from what I've witnessed in my brief stay here anyway. Here, we have a lot of equality. Go to the car park at a random Friday livestock sale and try to pick out the truck belonging to the wealthiest guy in the ring. You couldn't. Chris and I aren't seen as paupers or peasants with our 2006 Hilux, which has a wing mirror held on by gaffer tape and so many dents that it looks like a jealous ex has gone to town on it with a baseball bat. No one looks twice at you for having dirt under your fingernails, missing a shirt button or stinking to high heaven. That's almost the uniform. And you certainly aren't regarded as bottom of the food chain for being skint.

Our clapped-out truck has four lights on the dash at any given time. Its bumper is held on with cable ties. It's covered with war wounds and scars from collisions with gateposts and fences or from being scratched by Highland cattle's horns. All our clothes are threadbare and most likely have a tear or two. But, hey, we fit in just fine. (And distressed denim is a current trend, isn't it?) If times are tough, almost everyone around you will have been where you are, some for longer periods than others. And if the price of cattle plummets it will affect everyone – to varying degrees for sure, but all will feel it or feel the knock-on effect. That knowledge creates a real sense of camaraderie.

Chris and I started out with nothing – but as soon as I use that expression, I imagine people rolling their eyes. It sounds like some kind of *X Factor* sob story to pull at your heartstrings, except that it's not an exaggeration. It's true. We didn't own a trough or a trailer. We didn't have any sheep hurdles. We weren't registered with a farm vet. We knew that if we were to have a go at farming together as a full-time commitment, with no salary for me from my London job, we would have to save money, live from hand to mouth and still find a way to thrive while we did it. Sticking to a budget isn't the sexiest topic, but it's something that lots of couples argue over so partners really have to be on the same page with finances. And when you're making major life changes, it's crucial. For me, the unkindest cut of all was kicking the habit of my daily iced coffee with a shot of caramel syrup. It was my little snatch of luxury, a small reminder of my old life and that I *am* still fabulous, no matter how many types of shit I'm splattered with. I felt the sting – but I knew it had to go. And that was only the beginning.

Our first little flock for our first rented field consisted of those thirty-two pregnant ewes, the Suffolk Mules.

They cost us £69.50 per head, and when they lambed the following March, we had two options. We could keep the female lambs (ewe lambs) to breed from (except they wouldn't likely be sexually mature enough that coming autumn but the following one, so we'd have all those mouths to feed without a return for eighteen months). Or we could fatten the mothers and the lambs at the same time on autumn cover crops, like turnips, send them to market together and replace them with cull ewes ready for breeding the following year.

We went for cull ewes, which can cost as little as a fiver (basically the price of a posh coffee in Soho) while prime breeding ewes cost maybe £80 to £100. Culls have been dropped from another flock and sold, but you never know exactly why and it's rarely obvious. Sometimes a sheep has missing teeth (which stops her eating well). Maybe her udder's not soft (a 'lumpy bag') so she'll have problems feeding lambs. Her whole bag might even be bad. Or perhaps she's been a terrible mother and her lambs end up having to be cared for. (This happens: not all ewes take to it.) Chris would stand in the auction on a Tuesday and basically gamble. Would a cull ewe go lame after a couple of weeks? Would she develop some problem we'd missed that would suddenly make it obvious why she'd been kicked out of her previous flock? Would she not put on weight because she had no teeth to eat the fodder beet in the winter?

Our new cull ewes were given major TLC once they

arrived back at our farm, and in most cases they got to see the ram. After all, back before humans started meddling with sheep breeding, ewes would be cycling and falling pregnant until Nature decided they couldn't do it any longer. Even if we ended up with a few more orphans in the pet pen because the mother wasn't milky enough, it's not a bad profit if a five-pound cull ewe goes on to have a set of twins averaging £100 each.

This strategy won't make us millionaires any time soon. But it's how we've managed to increase our flock from thirty-two to 650 in five years with very little starter capital. It's not a conventional approach and we roll the dice with every lambing and every purchase. It's not uncommon to be down to our last five hundred pounds in the bank account, though, so we feel incredibly fortunate to have a roof over our heads that doesn't mind if we're short one month – or two. (Big thanks, Chris's mum and stepdad.)

The reality is we'll never be well off. (I sometimes wonder if Chris would be tempted to trade me in for fifty acres of clover if he got the chance: it's top grub for fattening lambs. But I'm sure he wouldn't really. Well – most days I'm sure.) Anyway, once you've accepted that living hand to mouth is okay and that plenty of happy families get along like this, everything is fine. Mostly. We're rich for a few months of the year, but those cheques from the market have to see us through until the next autumn. Some months we have only outgoings – which is bloody scary. The money stress is chronic and hor-rendous. I've learned that if you can't deal with it then farming's not for you.

Livestock and Mother Nature don't go easy on you if – like Chris – you have an autoimmune condition. They aren't kind and understanding if I'm having a down day about losing my dad. We can't dwell on the what-ifs: there's so much we can't control. A good community of friends and family around us for backup is a privil-ege both of us have – but it's also down to us to make it work. We have to find a flow and a rhythm – and hope we can pull it out of the bag. So far, that's what we've managed to do.

The rhythm of old friendships has changed too. Of course I still hang out with people I was close to before I was a farmer, but not everyone understands just how different life is now, and how much my priorities have altered.

'Okay. Got to go and feed the calves now,' I said. Chris and I were at a house-warming party, and it was my turn to stay sober: a pretty weird feeling when everyone around you is doing honey tequila shots.

'*Nooooo!*'

'No, you don't, Zo!'

'You gotta stay here with us!'

I'd already stopped off to fill the calves' water trough on the way to the party and done a full-on 'farm fashion' arrival, rocking Muck Boots under my silk kaftan (not a look you see every day) and traipsing mud across the room.

'I'll come with you if you want!' said my friend Naomi, enthusiastically.

I nearly choked on my mocktail. 'Are you sure?'

'Yeah! Course I'm sure! I'd love to!'

She'd had a few, and even if she hadn't, I would have said she was the least likely person voluntarily to set foot on a farm. But she was insistent. *Okay*, I thought. *So it's drunk plus one doing the next calf-feeding*. Twenty minutes on from our game of beer pong, we were in the yard. The second I appeared, all our calves started bellowing hungrily.

'Oh, my God!' cried Naomi. I picked up the huge bucket and began scooping powder into it. Her face fell. 'Um – don't they drink milk?' she asked me.

'Nope. I need to mix this up with water.'

'Don't you give them bottles?'

'No. They drink from here. It's got teats on it, look.' I knew exactly what she was thinking. This wasn't going to be the Instagrammable moment she'd been expecting.

Hungry calves will suck at anything. One caught the edge of her dress and dragged it into its mouth, making Naomi squeak with surprise as she tried to pull it out. 'It nearly sucked my finger off! I practically lost my ring! My God – its tongue! It's really rough!'

Next she tried to take a calf selfie, but it gave her face a huge slobbery lick, covering her with saliva.

'That's you with worms, then!' I said. I was joking, but couldn't help smiling at her horrified expression.

'Oh, Christ, Zo. Now it's doing a shit.'

'Welcome to the dream,' I told her.

'Can I wash my hands?'

'Here you go.' As we got back into the truck, I opened the glovebox and chucked her a wet wipe. For the duration of the drive, I could see her out of the corner of my eye, cleaning under every perfectly manicured nail. I wondered if she'd ever offer to help me again. Somehow, I didn't think she would.

* * *

'Merry Christmas, babe!'

'Merry Christmas, darlin'!'

A few weeks before, I'd spent my first full-time farming birthday worming lambs. Now it was 25 December. The alarm still went off at 6 a.m. It was pitch black outside. I remembered my Christmas mornings past, opening bottles of Moët and eating warm pains aux raisins. But now the animals needed to be fed, the water troughs had to be cleaned and that was that. It's the days when everybody else is on holiday that the reality of farming life really bites hard.

Of course Christmas Day is still a little bit special. Chris got to play Goat Santa that morning: it's his favourite job and they go mental for sprouts, so he headed off to the shed clutching the long stalks with sprouts growing on them. If you're a goat, Christmas treats don't come any better. Cows would rather have carrots or parsnips, but everybody had a special breakfast. When my mum, sister and their dogs arrived, we went on a Christmas walk-around. Once that was done, we opened our presents on hay bales in the barn and made sure we took an Insta-worthy sheep-in-a-Santa-hat photo: most farmers do that at Christmas, these days. Everyone was fine so I could head off to spend the day with my family while Chris stayed to celebrate with his. But if anything came up on the farm at any time, we knew we'd need to drop whatever festive thing we were doing and fix it. Our animals didn't care what day it was.

* * *

Okay – so our friends were moving forward and ticking off those big life milestones. As for my milestones – the ones I'd dreamed about through all my adolescence, the ones that had been on the Plan – a part of me was struggling not to feel envious, and was desperate to move to the next milestone with Chris. It felt like we were stuck in a rut when it came to progressing 'us'. Our relationship was always on the back-burner while the farm took precedence. Sometimes I even felt that our choices were inferior to those of my friends who were getting proposed to and signing their mortgage agreements.

It took time for me to become more comfortable with the idea of *not knowing* about the future, and to feel excited by the prospect of not being certain about what each day might bring. At that point, I was elated to have offloaded the heavy weight of failure from my shoulders, grateful to be free, like taking off your sweaty bra at the end of a heavy day. The biggest lesson I'd learned was not to take myself too seriously: a good sense of humour is key to survival.

I was comfortable in my London lifestyle and career – and in my own skin, too. But is comfortable always the best way to get the most out of the life we're given? For some, the answer may be yes. But I needed to be pushed, to widen the boundaries of what I could handle. In being swept out of my comfort zone and landing in a new life, I've discovered that I'm a warrior, not just a worrier. When you've survived bad times, you know that you could dig deep and do again what you did before if – God forbid – you ever had to.

So, gradually, my eyes weren't so green with envy of my friends. I was becoming wrapped up in my own plot, enthralled by learning that it's impossible that cow farts are ruining the planet, like the papers are suggesting, and celebrating my calves having solid poos by WhatsApping a photo to Chris. And that's the biggest thing I've learned in my thirty years' spinning round the sun: there is no pressure to fall in love or be in love in the way films and TV, or indeed social media, show it to be. Chris may not hold his hand out to help me over gates – but does that mean he doesn't love me? It just means he knows I'm capable of doing it myself. Do I gush about him all over social media? No. But does that mean I love him less than the girl who posts photos of her boyfriend massaging her feet, saying, 'This one,' and a love heart emoji? Of course not. As soon as I stopped striving for romantic-novel love, I saw that was never what I needed. I just needed someone to tell me I was fit while I stood in my bra and knickers projectile-vomiting in the toilet of my two-bedroom flat in Stoke Newington. Don't see that scene in the films now, do you?

We aren't fussed about taking romantic trips to Paris or going on dates to Winter Wonderland. We're happy to make a day of electric fencing into a date by simply deciding it's a date and eating our packed lunches together. We make the most of a birthday by classing a new billy goat as the gift – at least that makes it slightly easier to swallow the cost. We're both singing from the same hymn sheet, and until that changes, there will be no grumbles. If one of us falters, the other needs to step up and fill in.

We've never really sat down and made a proper business plan or model for the whole thing, like rational people would. We've learned how to live on a shoestring. It's been hard work and sweat and it's all down to us. That felt intimidating and unnerving at first. Some days, it still does. Some may look down their noses at how we operate, and some may think we're stark raving mental – but it's just how we've been able to grow and make a life for ourselves. Right from the start, we've been a team and we've worked as a team – because we've had to. No one can string us up for that.

Renting land in the way we do sometimes makes me feel quite sad. It means we're never going to own a cutesy little thatched-cottage farm with a row of identical wellingtons on the doorstep for all the members of our picture-perfect family: it's way out of our price range. We won't be popping out in a gleaming Land Rover to check on the stock grazing in our scenic fields either, or sipping tea from a flask as we lean on a photogenic gate. That's the farming fantasy, and our real life doesn't measure up to it.

I must admit I dream about that lifestyle sometimes. It's the perfect escape from the laborious task of washing out the calves' water trough every morning because they seem to get a thrill from taking a shit in it. I'd also like to bet that the owners of that thatched-cottage farm have expensive posh water troughs that rest on a cradle: no struggling with buckets for them because the water can be tipped down the slats and refilled using only one finger. But it's not going to be that way for us.

There are other major drawbacks to renting. We drive around daily to carry out checks on all our sites – the parcels of land are twenty miles apart and sometimes more. We travel backwards and forwards making sure the water troughs are full and no one's trying to hang themselves in a bramble bush. That means diesel costs running at hundreds of pounds a week. At some times of the year, the whole lookering process takes us three hours or longer. But it's all we've ever known together, so we try not to grumble too much.

* * *

The owners of land are responsible for its upkeep: mowing, tending, keeping it fertile. Having tenants grazing their animals on it solves that problem for them. Sheep improve the quality of grass because, believe it or not, they have enzymes in their saliva. When they eat the grass, the crop digs its roots in more deeply in response, draws up more water and gets stronger. But putting our animals out to graze can also mean a lot of extra work for us as graziers: sometimes the land is not fenced or there are no water-pipes so we have to install electric fences and transport water every couple of days to top up the troughs. All this adds to our costs and time. We even grazed sheep in a solar park for a couple of years, which was an excellent deal for the owners: without our animals to keep the grass down, they would have had to hand-mow around the panels. But the sheep kept on running underneath them, which was absolutely maddening. And, of course, although the owners of land receive subsidies from the government, as renters (even though our work helps to maintain it) we don't see any of it.

The subject of grazing can really get inside your head. Once when we were at a party I heard Chris across the room warming to the topic: he was waving his arms in the air, all set for a deep dive into the intricate details of the task that takes up a lot of his time. From a hasty glance at his listeners, I saw they had fixed, polite smiles and glazed eyes. I hurried across and gave him a quick little kick in the shin. 'Babe!' I muttered. 'Babe! No one cares!' This stuff's only fascinating if you're a farmer. Chris's face fell.

I already described how my internal strategist some-times freaks out about the future. I accept that we won't be able to afford our own farm – never say never, I suppose, but having that kind of money to spend is unlikely. What bothers me most is that I just have to have faith that a farm tenancy that allows us to hold all our land and animals in one place will come up for us. Some tenancies have con-tracts for ninety-nine years; if it happens, we could still find security, and it would certainly be a big improvement on the spread of rented fields in different places that we have now. There's a lot of change taking place in agriculture at the moment, and we're hoping that some existing tenants will start to retire. That way, fresh blood coming into the industry, like us, will stand a better chance of having their own tenancy. That's the dream – but tenancies on close to a thousand acres don't come up in the Garden of England all that often. So – who knows? I just remind myself that no one – no one at all – controls the future.

This is why, every time I blow out a birthday candle

or catch a dandelion fairy, I don't wish to win the lottery, or for eternal life, but just for a house with a farm where we can keep our amazing, feisty, fascinating, beautiful animals all together. Oh – and as many dogs as I want.

* * *

But what about the biggest milestone of them all – having a baby? Whether it's true or not, motherhood is considered to be a woman's central, life-defining decision. And babies had most certainly featured in my chocolate-box life plan. But I was in my late twenties, time was ticking and nothing was yet in place for me to make this dream a reality.

This is our big exception to the 'Hell, yeah – just do it' approach. It's worked in other areas, but we can't be impulsive here: we know that it just wouldn't be possible to live as we do, and take the risks we do, if we had a child who was reliant on us. Our finances all go into the farm so we live in Chris's family home. We couldn't bring up a child there – his mum and stepdad have been through quite enough with the orphan lambs and goat kids. As far as I know, you can't feed babies on sheep nuts and hay. So the bottom line was – and is – that, right now, we're not ready. Those are the cards we've been dealt.

Fact: I'm not getting any younger. My ovaries won't become more productive as the years go by. Will there ever be a good time for babies? Or even a not-quite-so-disastrous one? The answer is that I don't know. It's about finding a way to live with that. Sometimes I feel envious of women who get on with their lives, do their thing, then decide one day in their late thirties or even early forties that they're ready to have a family now and just . . . do it. No over-planning. No years of anxiety.

So where are we now? The eggs in my ovaries are dwindling, so I'm wondering if I should freeze them until the time is right. We've overcome so much. We've coped with not having staff and doing everything ourselves. We've worked around every single problem that's been thrown in our faces . . . but for me the final 'We've made it' moment would be going through the most natural and sacred act of them all: birth. I've spent years pulling lambs into the world, examining the mother's placenta. Just imagine sifting through your own to see the similarities. Cutting the cord that has connected a tiny living thing that I have grown and nurtured inside my belly for nine months. I want to reach down and pull that warm, wiggly being into the world.

I also know conception is – or can be – a bitch. Remember the episode of *Friends* when Monica and Chandler have sex at the hospital because she's ovulating and they have to do it *right now*? What if it ends up with a bit of how's-yer-father for Chris and me in the flatbed of the Toyota mid electric fencing, muddy overalls round our ankles and stakes poking where they shouldn't? Hardly part of the chocolate-box life plan.

It's when I start fretting about all this that I can really

lose sight of the positives. I forget that the way Chris and I have built a future for ourselves, working alongside one another 365 days a year, and yet still haven't killed each other, is a very big box we can tick. One which I'm both shocked at and proud of, in equal measure.

* * *

It's 6.05 a.m. Here I am on the tenth Sunday morning in a row, emptying the calves' trough bucket by bucket so as not to make the barn too waterlogged. My efforts are in vain as the roof has more holes in it than a colander, but if nothing else it's good for my core strength.

Even though I'd decided to leave London, I'd never truly fallen out of love with the world I used to live in. All jobs have their trying moments, but working in the salon was often exciting: I even met celebrities sometimes. I did hipster stuff – drank cocktails in Soho after work, went to gigs in Camden, hung out in a jazz bar on Carnaby Street, checked out limited-edition clothing brands and visited pop-up art galleries. In the end, though, I needed more air to breathe. Farming might be one of the most stressful, all-consuming lifestyles around – but it's also simple and pure.

Before I entered my new world, a sunshiny afternoon meant working on my tan out on the lawn in string bikini bottoms, or chilling in a pub garden sipping ice-cold Pimm's. Never did I think I'd see the day when I would look at the sunlight pouring down on the fields and feel delighted at the flourishing grass that will fatten my lambs. But these days, my mindset of happiness has changed, giving me faith that this happiness can be enough for me. *And now we're farming.*

Ram Bam

'Sheep die for kicks, Zo,' Chris said to me, one morning, as we started our inspection of the fields.

'My God, babe. That is *dark*.'

'Well – yeah. Yeah, it is. But it's like – Death really loves them. Remember that, if we find there's been an accident. No matter what we do, it's like their favourite pastime is to die.'

He was right. Sheep love to die – so much so that when you apply for your holding number (a unique number issued to livestock farmers to identify a specific parcel of land; it's mandatory to have one in order to keep sheep), they should also hand out a leaflet warning you that you aren't a bad shepherd or failing in your job when it happens. It's just their main ambition in life. It's what they do.

They must get extra 'lad points' if they die in the most random and unexpected way possible because that seems to be the goal: drowning in a puddle, choking on their own afterbirth, suffocating on a feed bag, killed by a falling tree branch. Think of the most absurd scenario you can and I can guarantee there'll be a sheep farmer in a dingy pub somewhere, propping up the bar and telling a similar tale. The best one I ever heard was someone coming down to breakfast one morning and finding a dead ewe with her head stuck in the cat flap. Unbelievable.

Don't get me wrong, I've had times when I've ugly-cried, hunched over a body in the pouring rain. I've lain awake at night fretting about whether I could have prevented the death from happening. But this really is Rule One of sheep farming: sheep love to die. What helps me most at times like that is knowing in my heart of hearts I've tried absolutely everything in my power to help each animal live, even if I've ended up losing them. And they've lived bloody good lives of open fields and full bellies. Beyond that, I know there's nothing more I could have done.

* * *

What winter means for a hairdresser: cute hats, cosy oversized knits, tights and a chunky boot, sipping hot chocolate with a shot of Kahlúa and fewer baby blonde highlights to put in. (That's very much a springtime kind of thing. People tend to darken their hair in the colder months.)

What winter means for a farmer: cramming all the chores into the limited daylight hours, my washing-machine having to work overtime, impossibly chapped lips, thinking of buying shares in Marks & Spencer's thermals, getting chilblains, looking like the son my father never had for months on end so that when I emerge from the shower Chris's eyes are on stalks as he remembers I'm not the prepubescent lad I've resembled around the yard all day. The only real positive about winter that I can think of is that your sandwiches don't get warm in the truck, meaning lunch doesn't need to be eaten by midday.

What you definitely feel in cold weather is vulnerable, at the mercy of Mother Nature. Of course, that's what you always are – but in winter it's a bit more fraught. It could be just a lack of vitamin D. Or perhaps it's because you're trudging through the mud every single fucking day. Thick, heavy mud that cakes everything you own, including your dog, which means you're battling with mud in your house as well as outside. It sucks at your soul. Death by mud.

When spring comes and you feel the constant mud skirmish subsiding, it's like being reborn. Spring is the season of new life and hope. You're a beautiful butterfly, able to open its wings after being swaddled in thermals, fleeces and overalls for months on end. The clocks go forward, which allows you a longer time frame to get your to-do list ticked off. You welcome the dewy mornings and warmth on your face with open arms, like a long-lost friend. Just jumping into the truck at dawn and driving away without having to scramble around for something to scrape the ice off the windscreen feels revolutionary. Coats are thinner; gloves and hats are retired to the glove-box. You can smell the heady cocktail of sun cream, lanolin and sweat carried on the breeze.

And then there's lambing.

Lambing is farming's crack cocaine – its highest high, and super-addictive. Once you've tried it, it's very hard indeed to walk away. Those new-lamb endorphins go whizzing round your body, bringing the warm, comforting feeling you last had when your favourite teacher gave you a wet paper towel and a custard cream after you fell over in the playground. It's a completely fresh experience every time, and it brings the deepest sense of purpose you've felt in all your years on Earth.

I remember one morning in the back apple orchard, noticing that one of our ewes was in distress as I did my early-morning checks. Sunset and sunrise are the times most lambs are born, and it was just after dawn. As low mist swirled around the trees, the scene looked like something out of *The Lord of the Rings*. This girl's back was marked in red to show she was having twins, so behind her stuck lamb must be another. The first one's head had been delivered, but now it was stuck, its face badly swollen with the pressure and its dark purple tongue poking out. But there was no need for panicked calls to Chris this time: I was pretty sure I could handle it.

First of all, though, I had to catch her – and even at a time like this, sheep can still move fast. But I managed it on the first attempt – which shows how far I'd come. I pushed the ewe gently but firmly to the ground and slipped my hand inside her above the lamb's head. Chris says my small hands are my secret lambing weapon: I can get into spaces where bigger fingers can't, and I'm nimble up there.

The lamb's front legs were right back, which was how it had got stuck. I felt its shoulder blade then followed down one leg towards the bend. Once I got hold of that, I could ease the leg forward, and a hoof popped out, taking some of the pressure off the lamb's neck. Pulling on that hoof and on the head might deliver it – but it would take a lot of force and I remembered learning very early on in my career as a shepherd what could go wrong if I tried that. Another trick is to put two fingers up the ewe's bumhole and push down to make more space for the delivery. But there was an easier way: I slid my hand back inside her, and gently eased the lamb's second leg forward. Once it was presenting in Superman position – one head, two hoofs – it was delivered quickly. The newborn looked just like a grumpy old man with its fluffy, bushy eyebrows – these twins had obviously been fathered by the Southdown ram. I pulled it around to its mother to sniff and lick. Then as she tried to clamber to her feet, the second lamb shot out of her like a missile, taking me completely by surprise. It was much smaller – and a whole lot more streamlined. I looked at it lying motionless on the ground, not even sure it was alive. It was absolutely bald and its tiny body was so pink.

Shit. There must be something wrong with it. Why hasn't it grown a fleece? Perhaps its body hasn't quite formed. Perhaps she's had a live lamb and somehow miscarried the other at the same time. That's weird – at least she'll have one to look after. But now the second lamb was twitching and trying to hold its wobbly head up. Best not to interfere, because if you get too involved with newborns, it can cause their mothers to reject them. I think this might be because they smell of humans if they've been touched too much. Or perhaps it's just the presence of the shepherd interfering with their bonding. I left the new mum to get on with it.

As she licked off its yellowish birth goo, I realized why this lamb twin was so unlike the other. *Oh, my God – it's a whole different breed!* It must have been fathered by the Charollais ram, and Charollais lambs look like little naked mole rats, with no fleece. If the spring sun is too strong, they can even get sunburned ears. Now the ewe was proudly licking and bonding with both her new lambs. *She's only gone and had twins from two different dads!*

I shouldn't have been so surprised: with a large flock and a choice of rams, it's not that uncommon. A ram can cover – which means impregnate – more than fifty ewes in a very short timespan. At lightning speed, more often than not. That's why when you buy a ram, you need to make sure that the lad's in tip-top shape for the busy weeks to follow.

We paint each ram so that we know just where he's been and which ewes he's mated. We mix coloured powder and veggie oil to make 'raddle paint' and slap it on their chests (brisket), which is an incredibly messy job, and then we let the testosterone-riddled, randy bastards loose in a field full of potential conquests to sow their seed. When each ram mounts a ewe, he leaves a coloured stain on her bum, and when you check the flock on the first morning after you've put the rams in, it's breathtaking. A carpet of coloured bums – promiscuous is a massive understatement when it comes to sheep. You also get a few ewes who'll go on chasing the rams, like groupies, even though they're already covered with raddle paint. Waking up the-morning-after-the-night-before and having a steaming hot shower to wash away your mistakes isn't going to cut it for those girls.

Before I was a farmer, I never gave much thought to why lambs were always born in the springtime, or why all the Easter cards had fluffy lambs and daffodils printed on them. Just . . . Nature's way, maybe? But hang on – what's stopping sheep breeding all year round? Other animals do. The realization that it was all a well-orchestrated plan on the farmers' part was a light-bulb moment for me. That's the timing we use: start shagging on Bonfire Night and the orgy basically lasts until all the ewes are pregnant; 5 November is 147 days before April begins, and that's exactly how long the average pregnancy for a sheep takes. Nice and easy to remember.

Rams are very full-on indeed, and extremely persistent. Watching them in action makes you thankful that male humans (mostly) have mastered seduction techniques a little better. But the ewe won't stand and take it unless she's ready (ovulating), so the girls do get to choose. She starts giving off hormones that make the boys want to sniff her wee, and the rams lift their top lips to take full advantage – that's where their scent glands are. Once a ewe has a candidate in mind, she backs up to him and wags her tail, which basically spreads the scent further to entice him in, like us spraying a bit of Coco Chanel before a date.

You know when it gets near closing at a grotty club and suddenly the mood changes? The stragglers' time to pull is running out and the pulling gets sloppy – no time for chat-up lines, winks or casual arm grazes, just straight to grinding to Sean Paul like your life depends on it. Well, it's pretty much like that. The ram is in a frenzy by now, licking his lips frantically, making the ugliest of grunting noises and using a front leg to stroke her in a very over-whelming manner. Then two pumps and a grunt, and it's on to the next tail-wagging maiden. Like sex addicts in a brothel. It's completely primitive.

A ewe cycles every sixteen days and, ideally, a farmer wants them to cycle together, or 'sync'. That means they'll come into season at a similar time, soon after the rams go in. Otherwise you'll be lambing for months on end because they've all been served over such a vast stretch of time and sometimes over multiple cycles. Some farmers absolutely nail the whole process and within a few weeks everyone's lambed so they'll all be ready to go to market at a similar time – which means a large cash injection for the farm. But this kind of coordination takes practice. Right now, we're still working on it.

Still, we're learning all the time. These days, we almost always 'flush' our ewes, which mainly means putting them on lush grass. The healthier they are, the more fertile they become because they know there's enough grub to sustain them and grow their lambs (a bit like humans having more sex on holiday). The happier and healthier the sheep, the more eggs are released so more can be fertilized and more twins and triplets will be born.

Another common practice is to use a 'teaser ram'. He'll be intact which means he hasn't been castrated and still smells like a ram, but his tubes will have been tied so he'll never impregnate anyone. The teasers run round the ewes causing a huge scene, like kids in a sweet shop, and getting the girls hot under the collar, horny and riled up before the real rams come to town. Another common practice, but a little more of a faff, is 'sponging'. A tampon-like object is entered into each ewe's vagina for around two weeks or more, often alongside an injection to sync their cycles and give them an extra little boost. It's a system of farming that works for a lot of farms up and down the country but we don't do it. It's too costly and, for us, too unnatural.

And there's another question. When do you step back and let your animals be – as they would live in the wild – and when do you intervene and 'farm' them? It's a subject I battle with often – almost daily. Finding the balance is something I'm still working on. Learning about the different practices in different cultures and set-ups is the best way to make an informed decision about how much you want to meddle in their existence.

* * *

It was the middle of the lambing season. By 2 p.m., we'd been up and on our feet for ten hours.

'She's not a bloody Christmas turkey, Christopher!' I snapped.

I knew I was skating on thin ice but I was too worn out to check that my filter was working properly. When you're that tired, manners go out of the window. Chris was looking really annoyed – I reckoned he was 0.5 seconds from walking away and leaving me to cope with this lambing emergency on my own.

The ewe had a prolapse – the fourth I'd seen that spring. There was a bright red bulge of flesh at the entrance to her vagina where her birth canal had been expelled while over-straining during lambing, or sometimes this can be caused by a really outsized lamb. Whatever the reason, a prolapse blocks the way so the lamb can't be delivered. A sheep might have been removed from her flock because of a history of developing this condition, so it's part of the risk when we buy cull ewes: if it's happened once, it's likely it will happen again. Once we know, we'll mark her back with a big black cross: that way, we won't try to breed from her again and she can go to fatten up on turnips.

We'd already washed the protruding parts of her vagina and uterus with warm water and sugar to help them shrink. Now they'd hopefully fit back inside her – it was just getting them in there that was the problem. I'd been reading up on this and wanted to try a new method I'd heard about, but I'd need to lift the ewe's back legs to do it and she weighed 80 kilos at least so Chris would have to help me. Except he didn't want to and he thought he knew best. It was pissing me off that I couldn't have a go on my own, but I just wasn't strong enough.

He'd been trying to stuff her insides back, like a turkey ready for roasting, and she was kicking and wriggling, understandably, given her situation. Each time he shoved her uterus into place, it popped right out again. We'd already had two tries. This must have been awful for the ewe, and I suddenly felt the prickle of tears. My lips were shaking.

I screamed at Chris again. *'You're being so rough!'* He'd had enough by now and he walked away muttering something about me being crazy. That made me so angry that it gave me a surge of extra strength and I managed to hoick up the ewe just high enough to get gravity to help me. In went her uterus, just like I'd thought it would, and before she could expel it yet again, I managed to insert what's called a prolapse spoon to keep it in place. It's a little plastic gadget that looks like a tiny capital T, secured to the animal's wool, with a tongue resting in her vagina to stop her straining too hard.

The motto of this story is to eat up all your spinach like Popeye when you're looking after sheep. That way, you can replace prolapses on your own so you won't have to ask your boyfriend for help.

* * *

Once the girls are all 'covered' they're left alone over the winter. We make sure they're well fed with fodder beet, a root vegetable like a turnip, and plenty of hay in round metal frames with a tarpaulin roof to keep it dry. Then, as winter starts to subside (hopefully), we scan the pregnant ewes. Imagine a human ultrasound at the maternity unit, except that this is carried out in a muddy field and the mums-to-be don't receive a printout photo to post on Instagram with a pair of booties and a 'Soon To Be Three' hashtag. But, for us, seeing the progress of the pregnancies is when we really start to feel excited.

Gathering ewes when they're only a month or two away from giving birth is slower-paced than usual. We have to make sure they don't bang into each other and flock together too tightly. Then, one by one, they walk or waddle up a small ramp and stand so that Malcolm, our scanner (he used the same hand-held device to ultrasound his pregnant wife, the only difference being that he didn't have to apologize to the sheep for rubbing on cold gel), can put the probe under its belly and see on the screen how many heartbeats there are.

Every single year I'm hopeful that I'll be able to differentiate between the foetuses and other blurry shapes on the screen – and every year I'm disappointed that I can't. Malcolm always knows, and he can identify single, twin or triplet pregnancies. We then mark each ewe with a coloured dot so that we can feed her accordingly: blue for single, red for twins, and an orange line for triplets. These colours are incredibly important for many reasons, the most important being that each mother-to-be must receive the right nutrition. Without it, ewes can become very sick because the growing lambs take all the nutrients from their bodies, and they develop twin-lamb disease (also known as pregnancy toxaemia): this is when the ewe's body fats become an energy source, which creates toxic by-products.

Twin-lamb is relatively easy to spot if you know what you're looking for: the main sign of trouble is any ewe that's separated from the flock. Then, as you get up close to the patient, she seems wobbly and blind or away with the fairies – a condition we call 'stargazing'. Another telling sign is her breath: no farm animal's breath smells good but if she's suffering from twin-lamb you'll smell pear drops a mile off. It's caused by ketones building up in her body, a sign that she hasn't been grazing properly. Ketosis can damage her and her lambs if she's not treated. We have a handful of these cases every year, and no matter how carefully we watch for the signs, we lose one or two ewes and their unborn lambs. If we see on the scanner that a ewe isn't pregnant, she tends to be sold as mutton so the short supply of winter grass can be eaten by the pregnant ewes that need it.

Another reason for marking up the expectant mothers is that once the lambs are arriving, the chaos seems a bit less overwhelming if we know exactly what's going on. Anything to make your life easier when you're in the thick of lambing season! If you spot a ewe going into labour and she's marked with a blue dot (single) but looks like she's got a lot of milk and is strong, we aim to 'graft' a second lamb onto her to rear as her own. This is meddling with Mother Nature (again) – but my reasoning is that it's just being resourceful and she's got two teats for a reason! We place an orphan lamb underneath her during her final few contractions so that the new lamb is born on top of it and it gets covered in birth fluids. Orphan lambs' mothers have died or rejected them – not all ewes take to motherhood – and the lamb has to be very young, less than three or four days old: once it has had bottle feeds, it's difficult to get it to search for a teat or to suckle. We wrap it in the new lamb's birth sac and when the mother starts licking and bonding with the new arrival, she starts believing (hopefully) that both are her offspring. Sometimes, if the orphan is a little feisty, we even tie its legs together with baling twine so that it's shaky on its feet, like a newborn. Once its newly arrived sibling can stand up, we untie the bow and, hey presto, twins.

If the mother's still not completely sold on the twins idea, we get Indie on the case: hopefully the presence of a 'predator' ignites the ewe's protective maternal instincts. It's rare that this fails. Once she starts stamping at the dog to protect her young, we're doing well. A lamb latching onto its adoptive mum as she pushes it onto her teat is a sight to behold after all the stress and apprehension of dealing with an orphan. A new family is bonding.

We lamb really intensively for around six weeks on average, and then everything calms down. It's the best time in the world, not only for the adrenalin of the moment, but for the thrill of witnessing new life. But, of course, there are deep lows too. Where there's live-stock, there's deadstock. (God, how I *hate* it when people say that – as if it's going to comfort you even remotely.) A shepherd can go from elation, because she's managed to manoeuvre a lamb around within a womb and deliver it safely, to devastation because another that seemed to be doing well has suddenly dropped dead.

You shed a quick tear, eat a Kinder Bueno, and then on you go. You can never stop for long.

* * *

It was boiling hot and muggy. The farm felt more like the Sahara than the North Downs in spring. We were towards the end of lambing but we had a ewe still pregnant: she'd been caught by the ram fairly late. She looked listless and mopey – definitely not quite herself – and was due any day, so we were keeping an eye on her.

Early one morning I noticed a browny-pink discharge under her tail. 'It means the lamb's died, Zo,' Chris told me.

'Definitely?'

'Yep. For sure. She'll need to get it out today or else it's going to kill her.'

'Delivered like normal except dead?'

'I hope so,' he said. 'But her fluids will have dried up and she won't get her contractions so strongly.' For a quick birth, everything needs to be quite slippery, but once the lamb has died and a few hours have passed, there's very little amniotic fluid left to lubricate the foetus for delivery.

In the early afternoon, I returned on my own to check the ewe again. By now she was straining to deliver. She was going to need some help so I went to get the calving gloves, which fit right up to your shoulder, because whatever had caused the death of her lamb – infection, disease – I knew it could be dangerous to come into contact with it. There's a risk of spreading it to the other ewes, and even pregnant women are at risk from infections in sheep, whose fluids can carry bacteria that cause miscarriages. No one who is having a baby, or even some-one trying to conceive, should ever assist with lambing.

Once I'd got my gloves on, I had to catch the ewe so I could help her birth the lamb – although she was dis-tressed, she was still giving me the runaround. Some sheep will just lie down and let you help, but this one was feisty and feral. Feral sheep are wilder and harder to contain: that's why she hadn't been colour-sprayed, so I couldn't be sure how many lambs she had in there. Her wild instincts weren't helping her now, though: after fif-teen minutes' chasing after her in the raging midday heat, I felt dizzy. I needed our shepherd's crook – a long curved tool a bit like a walking stick with a clip on one end – to give me that extra metre's reach so I could grab a back leg. I knew exactly where it was: in Chris's truck. Boiling, sweaty and annoyed, I left a testy voicemail on his phone, wondering why it was there and not where I needed it.

Finally, I managed to grab the struggling ewe and open the tailgate of the livestock trailer. I guided her in by the horns, still objecting, but at least now she couldn't run away. The trailer is metal – even hotter than the field – and the moment we were in there, I was almost knocked out by a vile, eye-watering smell. This lamb wasn't just dead: it was rotting inside her.

I raced over to the fridge in the barn. That's where we keep a stash of oxytocin: a drug that makes the uterus contract and helps labour to progress. (We store some gin in the same fridge and, at that moment, I was tempted.)

In front of the cool open door, I took a moment, wiped my face and tried to gather my thoughts. This ewe was going to lose her lamb. Perhaps, if I tried to introduce one, she might adopt. But, no, that couldn't work: there wouldn't be a whole dead lamb to skin, and that's the only chance you have of making this happen.

It sounds brutal, but a lamb that's been born whole but has died can be skinned with a very sharp knife (it takes a lot of skill and practice), starting with an incision around the neck – you have to be very careful not to cut the flesh – then peeling off the skin like you would a satsuma. Then you fetch an orphan lamb and dress it in your masterpiece – like a onesie. The most important parts to get into position are the arsehole and the umbilical cord because that's where the ewe will sniff most. You pen the lamb with the potential mother in the hope that it smells right to her and she will adopt it.

Most adoptive mothers are a little unsure at first, depending on how long they were with their original lamb and if it ever made a noise, but in most cases they will take on the new one. Once they're getting into motherhood and before the flesh on the inside of the lambskin onesie starts stinking, you remove it and the lamb-ewe bond will be unbreakable.

The first time I watched Chris in action with the skinning knife, I thought, *Fat chance I'll ever be doing THIS!* But when you're faced with a ewe standing over her dead lamb and calling and calling for it, and you suddenly realize you might be able to heal her distress *and* get an orphan looked after, it's astounding what you can pull out of the bag.

The first time I ever skinned a lamb alone was in spring 2020, when Chris was suffering from an autoimmune flare-up and I was doing an early-morning check. I found a dead lamb on the ground; it had just been delivered. I'd watched him do it and I'd helped, so I felt that I knew what I was doing. My lamb onesie wouldn't have won any prizes but it did the job, and the ewe whose lamb had died bonded happily with a twin whose mother was struggling to produce enough milk.

If I could have tried the onesie trick with this girl I would have, but there'd be no amniotic fluid to fool her and her lamb was decomposing, so no chance of getting its skin. All I could do was run back and give her an injection to – hopefully – help open her cervix. *In twenty minutes or so, there's a chance she'll expel the body.*

Twenty minutes went by and there was no sign that the oxytocin was working. By now my stomach was sinking. The only option left was to deliver the lamb myself. I put my hand inside her, and everything was dry. I tentatively reached higher, until I was touching the dead lamb. I wanted to move it into Superman position to ease it down and out, but the front leg came away from its body the moment I pulled. I'd have to deliver it in pieces.

Over and over again, gagging and sweating, I went back in for the next segment – a front leg, a back leg, bits of skin – and the next. It took forty-five minutes before I was sure I had all of the lamb's body. Each piece I pulled out fell apart in my hands, exactly like cooked aubergine, soft and fibrous. The mother was lying down, head back, doing feeble little pushes and grinding her teeth. The scene was bloody awful, like something from a horror film, and the only way to override the grimness was to focus on helping the ewe: she would die if I didn't do this properly. When it was over, she looked dazed. I gave her a handful of sheep nuts and a large injection of pain relief. We'd need to keep an eye on her for the next few days as she adjusted. There'd also be the risk of mastitis – infection in her teats – because the milk that had been waiting for the lamb wouldn't now be expressed.

But the most important thing to do was to get rid of the pieces of decomposing flesh. As she clambered shakily to her feet, I let her out of the trailer and walked back to the barn with a Tesco bag full of decaying lamb and afterbirth, to dispose of it all properly in case it was toxic to the other lambs and ewes. The smell from that bag was so intense that it stayed with me for hours afterwards – it was as if it had physically infected me, burning inside my nostrils. The hardest revulsion to overcome is a terrible smell: you gag and heave however hard you try not to. I breathed fresh air as deeply as I could, ate a Bueno and carried on.

It was evening when I checked the ewe again, and when I did, I could hardly believe what I saw. She was steady on her feet, and standing next to her, a bit wobbly and gooey but energetically sucking, was a newborn lamb. Behind the dead twin, she'd had a second, protected by its birth sac from the infection and decay of the first. Nature is incredible sometimes.

* * *

'We're going to kill her first, babe, right?'

My mouth was dry and my voice was shaking.

Chris didn't answer. He was already striding over to the truck, then I saw him heading back with his gun in the crook of his arm.

'Yes, Zo,' he told me. 'We'll be needing some dry towels.'

'Um – do you know where to cut?' I asked him.

'Yes,' he said briefly. 'Yes, I do.'

The cold early-spring weather that year meant our ewes could be susceptible to twin-lamb disease. As a sick ewe gets weaker, she loses her legs and can't stand, and once she's down, it's 50:50 whether you'll bring her round again. You have to work fast when you're dealing with these cases, and every farmer has their own little recipes and tricks, not all of which have official veterinary approval. If it works, though, and it's not causing harm or distress to the animal, it's a good 'un. When sheep are in ketosis, their livers are under a huge amount of strain so you must get as many vitamins and minerals into them as possible to support their organs; we use an injection. But in the last year or so, it's been difficult to source injectable vitamins because human bodybuilders have started using them and it's causing a national shortage.

Once the ewe's been jabbed, I give her some propylene glycol in a syrupy liquid down her throat, and follow it up with a Red Bull – flat ideally. After that, she gets plenty of water, and the vitamin and mineral mix that I make her drink every few hours. Then all I can do is cross my fingers. If she starts nibbling at her ivy (a firm favourite), you know you have a hope. But if she's down for longer than a day, her legs tend to give way. After that, all you can do is try to hold her up between your knees every few hours so that her legs can regain some strength.

This girl was down with twin-lamb, and nothing we did seemed to help. For days we'd been taking it in turns to drench her (squirt the vitamin potion down her throat) and to stand with her between our legs for twenty minutes at a time. We'd had a few moments of false hope when she seemed to be improving, but then it was pretty clear she wasn't, and now, after a conversation with our vet, we decided that if we didn't do something, we were going to lose three lives – hers and her twins'. Her milk had let down into her udder, which is called 'bagging up': it's a definite sign that she wasn't far off lambing, so the lambs would hopefully have developed enough to survive on their own if we delivered them by C-section.

Farmers work closely with vets and they're realistic and honest with us, especially regarding costs and the odds on good outcomes. Some farmers might get the emergency vet out to deliver these lambs, but for us that would add up to a very hefty bill, especially with the call-out charge on a Sunday. If it's already too late then there'd be the costs for disposal of three bodies. It wasn't worth the risk. If we were going to save these lambs, we'd have to do it ourselves.

We set about clearing an area to make it as sterile as possible in a barn, which is never going to be a very surgical environment. Then I went to the boot of the car and got some clean towels from my hairdressing kit while Chris sharpened his knife. If you had told blonde hairdresser Zoë that she would be spending her Sunday evening sober in a barn about to perform a C-section on a sheep, well, it's impossible to imagine her reaction. (The sober part might have been the most unlikely.)

I looked very intensely at the ewe to see if she knew what was coming. Her eyes were glazed. She was dying in front of us – I could see the life just draining away. One thing was for sure: she had no idea what was going on or what was about to happen. I held on to this thought as Chris loaded the gun. Once her heart had stopped beating, her lambs would be starved of oxygen. Unless we got them out immediately, there would be three deaths instead of one.

I held the towels ready for the newborns and Chris

made the incision on the bulge of her belly. Skilfully he cut through the muscle, pierced the sac and whipped out the lambs. As he handed each one to me, I dropped them to the ground to simulate the sensation of falling out of the mother during birth. That little knock usually brings a lamb round and then you can get to work swinging them by their back legs to make sure they have no fluid in their airways, rush the blood round their little bodies and get everything going. It worked, and a few minutes later, bedraggled and pumped full of adrenalin, we had two live lambs. They stumbled about like little Bambis, trying to suck anything and everything – my hands, my legs, my clothes. It was heartbreaking to see, but at least they were still with us. Two new and healthy lives in the pen.

* * *

Ah – the pure joy that is the pet pen: an oasis of little noses, wiggly tails and sticky poos. Bottle lambs, pet lambs, sock lambs, cades, orphans: the list of names they're called by is long and depends on whereabouts in the country you live. But all the different words mean the same: something that may look very cute but is far from ideal.

Besides the mum dying, there are lots of other reasons why a lamb goes into the pet pen. A ewe may have produced twins but has limited milk so she can't feed both. She may have rejected the lamb or had triplets (sheep have only two teats). If a lamb has been unwell and we've had to give it some kind of treatment, perhaps its mother won't accept it back. Any farmer will do everything in their power to leave a lamb on its mother: removal is the very last resort. Young animals are meant to have a mother raise them, and they'll do better on their mothers' milk. Substitute milks come in powdered form, but they're incredibly expensive and I feel the lambs never blossom as well on them: the mother's body meets the lamb's needs best. That's why the goal is always to adopt any of your bottle lambs onto a new mum as soon as possible.

The most frustrating situation is when a ewe has a perfectly healthy lamb and decides she doesn't fancy rearing it. Imagine if humans were in the birthing suite and suddenly announced to the midwife, 'Nah, no thanks. Changed my mind. Just not into this.' With sheep it's very rare, but it happens. Sometimes ewes just aren't maternal and turn out to be awful mothers – but at least there's a good chance with adoption. Goat mothers are much savvier: they don't fool easily and it's very difficult to get orphans adopted by other mothers. We've never even tried it.

It helps a bit to humanize the ewe if she rejects her lamb and just say to yourself, 'Well, it's not her fault. Perhaps she's going through some things . . .' but humanizing every scenario in farming isn't healthy. There's no reasoning with sheep. Some just aren't cut out to be mothers and that's that. After an incident like this, the ewe gets a black cross on her back and won't be allowed to try again.

It's lovely in the pet pen at first – a real novelty to have a bottle lamb or two to rear. That warm feeling of them *needing* you and waggling their tails when they hear your voice is enough to make even Chris go all gooey. But before long, mixing all the milk and bottle-feeding them every four hours, twenty-four hours a day becomes quite hard going. Uploading selfies and cute videos of 'feeding time at the zoo' starts to wear a bit thin. You find yourself on autopilot, holding a bottle with your eyes closed, knowing exactly which order you'll feed them, which rascal tries to push the others off the bottle and which likes to be held in your arms or he won't suckle. So, these days, we really get on it: we organize adoptions in every possible situation and do all we can to keep the hand-reared numbers down. This last spring, we had just four orphan lambs in the pen. It's a sure sign we're making progress as farmers.

* * *

'This one's going to be prem, Zo,' Chris said. 'It's way too soon. And she's not been that bothered about the lick bucket either.'

We always use lick buckets – containers full of vitamins and minerals that are tempting to sheep – to give our pregnant ewes as much support as possible, but if someone has the chance and won't lick, it's difficult to know what more we can do. And as one of our ewes went into labour early, things weren't looking good.

When Sunny was born, she was tiny: about the length of a Sky remote control. I was sure she was going to be dead. 'Zo, she can't survive,' Chris told me. 'There's just no way. We're better off helping her mother to recover.' But as I got closer, this minute little thing made a bleating sound and tried to lift her head. Then she gave me a stare that was absolutely packed with attitude. This was a lamb that wasn't giving up.

'She's so alert, babe,' I said. 'I really think she's having a try.' And if they do that, I can't give up on them.

Chris still thought she wouldn't make it: he reckoned her internal organs wouldn't be properly formed. But I took the miniature lamb into the shed and gave her some colostrum (the extra-rich milk a mother produces – humans too – in their offspring's earliest days to give them a kick-start. It's thick and creamy, almost like custard, and we call it liquid gold because it's got all the goodness and antibodies a lamb needs to thrive). I just knew – I'm not exactly sure how – that her determination would pay off. She was so premature that her hoofs were like jelly, almost the consistency of Haribo sweets. If a lamb's full term, its hoofs harden up as soon as it's born. She survived, and became our lucky charm. She wanted to live and I wanted her to live. What better partnership could there ever be?

* * *

Lambing is round-the-clock non-stop, and twenty-four hours after they've arrived, it's time to check on each of our newcomers. They're so little they can twist on a sixpence – and so nimble and fast, it's hard to believe. Turn. Sprint. Turn. It's a pretty full-on workout. Once we've caught them, we check that their umbilical cords, which we've sprayed with iodine when they're first born, are clean and dry so that no bacteria can get in. Then we make sure that everyone has a full tummy. If a lamb doesn't seem to be feeding well enough, I have to catch the mother and get things going. I stretch out alongside the ewe with my left hand holding her mouth, then with my right hand, I reach down and attach the lamb to a teat. Forget about Salute to the Sun, it's a whole new kind of yoga.

We number and ring each lamb, sticking a little rubber band (like an orange Cheerio) on their tails just below a V that's visible on the underside by their genitals. Within a few weeks the tail will fall off and the lamb will be less likely to have a mucky bum and fewer flies will therefore be attracted to it. For females, it's also cleaner for birthing. The same type of stretchy ring goes round the balls if the lamb is male, and means they won't reproduce or shag their mum or sister – remember just how randy sheep can be! Fun fact: whenever I've talked about castration on social media, I've got into some seriously weird conversations. These have always been with men who find the whole idea *waaay* too fascinating. Nope – I've no idea what that's about, and I'm not too sure I want to know. (Mind you, they're not as strange as the guys who keep asking me for photos of my bare muddy feet. #farmfeet. That's an OnlyFans idea right there.)

Once the lambs are banded, we spray a number on each and the same one on its mother, using red spray for twins and blue for singletons. If a mum and her twins are all labelled Red 22, it helps us spot any ewe who might be trying to steal another's lambs and also lets us easily re-unite any separated families. This sounds simple, but at the time it feels like such a chore: on four hours' sleep and a Wispa, there are forty-odd lambs to catch without a sheep-dog. But calm future Zoë will thank hyperventilating-hot-mess Zoë for sprinting up and down the fields in pursuit. We number them as we go along, and doing it at this stage makes us fool- and exhaustion-proof. It means that I can quickly phone Chris: 'I'm in the field with the pond and I've got a ewe with red 71 but no lambs. Have you seen them?' The alternative is us trying to describe individual sheep to each other, which has been tried and almost started the Third World War. How many ways can you think of to distinguish a sheep?

Lambing is a period like no other, addictive yet draining at the same time. That feeling you get when a lamb takes its first breath is like a drug and I could never get bored with the sound of new lambs finding their voices. In my pet pen, I can recognize each one. You are physically and mentally so spent, yet something drives you on and on, finding superhuman strength and resilience. Until suddenly it's the end and you get the blues because it's over for the year. That's when you find yourself sitting in bed at night looking through your camera roll and desperately trying to relive the moments.

I've tried explaining all of this, but it's hard to find the words to do it justice. Watching new life entering the world should be something that all children get a chance to do in school. Every human on Earth should witness it. If you get the chance, go to a lambing open day, when some farms welcome visitors. If you're lucky enough, you'll get to see the first divine moments of a creature's life. Being present at births and seeing animals take their final breath has had a huge impact on me. What could be more grounding than witnessing these things? A sheep has lived outside in the wind and rain, feeding on water and grass, and they've produced a new living, breathing being. Along with the heartache and the highs and lows, it's an incredible privilege to be a part of the process.

* * *

If a lamb goes missing, it's quite likely it will have been eaten. Our animals are always at risk, whether from foxes, badgers, crows and even flies. To begin with, this was something I hadn't anticipated. I knew we had to look after them and serve as their guardians, but we also have to kill for them too. I didn't expect that. Chris takes care of all vermin and predators on the farm, not because I'm opposed to doing it, but I don't have a gun licence: the shooting game isn't something that interests me. That's also why he handles casualties who sadly might need to be put down.

I'd seen city foxes in North London, scraggy and mange-ridden creatures raiding the bins and eating left-over doner kebabs off the ground. Towards the end of my time in the city, I spotted them most days and at night I'd hear their bloodcurdling mating shrieks. (No matter how many times you've heard them, a part of you still thinks it's a newborn baby getting snatched from its cot.) Country foxes are much healthier than those poor sods and the ones that live in the orchards at the farm are the most stunning copper colour (an 8.43 L'Oréal colour swatch, hairdresser Zoë can't help thinking). The morning sun reflects off those coats with a gloss I could only ever dream of getting on my old clients. Then, one evening, I found out why they look so well.

It was dusk and during the last checks before bed, I noticed a ewe in the corner of one of the back orchards acting out of sorts. There was nothing visible happen-ing yet, but I thought she was going to lamb that even-ing. Still, it could be hours so I went into the caravan to shower and grab something to eat. I knew Chris had discovered a rogue lamb's leg in the same field during the dawn checks, and he'd therefore decided to spend a few hours fox-shooting to protect the flock. But a part of me still felt that the foxes were doing what they needed to do to feed their young and survive. They were parents too. It's the circle of life.

When I went out again, it had grown dark and I took the torch with me. Just as I'd expected, the ewe was lambing up against the fence. She'd managed to deliver one of the twins herself and was licking it frantically. Then, as I checked them over, the beam of my torch caught a reflection just behind her. It was a pair of watching eyes, red and gleaming.

The fox was crouching less than a metre away from our brand new lamb. He was waiting for the second to be born, when the ewe would be briefly distracted from her firstborn – and that was when he would swipe it. It's common in the predator world. I drove him off that night – by now I was feeling so fiercely protective of our new lambs that it was less circle-of-life and more 'Let's get the shotgun.' But I know I can't be there every moment, with every single newborn. There's only so much that we can do.

Another risk to sheep is from dogs. Owners often seem to think their dog is somehow different, domesticated and tame, and that its instinct to hunt and to kill has disappeared. But it hasn't. Dogs are the descendants of wolves, and we've had loads of dog attacks on our farm. A golden retriever once escaped from someone's garden and ripped the throats out of half a dozen of our Hebrideans. One ewe it attacked was left alive but with half her face torn off, and I did everything I could to nurse her back to health, bathing her injuries every day and trying to keep them clean enough to heal. I thought she had a chance, but then she miscarried – this was a direct result of the trauma of the dog attack – and the early delivery of her lamb killed her in the night.

I was also deeply shocked by how much damage a badger can inflict. They were some of the cutest animals in the Sylvanian Families games and toys I loved when I was little, so how could they eat a ewe's udder while she was stuck on her back? I guess the thought of all that milk was just too tempting. (Not quite *The Wind in the Willows* now, is it?) The circle of life is a natural thing and it holds beauty. But it can also be savage. Even though we've all watched antelopes getting ripped apart on David Attenborough's TV shows, seeing it with your own eyes is something else. That's the moment when you understand what it really means to kill or to be killed.

* * *

Everyone assumes that because I'm a hairdresser I must immediately have become a straight-A shearer. I mean, Chief Shepherdess: from cutting hair to shearing sheep, right? Fat chance. I'm absolutely terrible at it, not for lack of trying. Eventually, though, I had to take the decision to leave this one to the experts.

Shearing cripples my back and causes me no end of

frustration, especially because it looks so easy when the professionals do it yet I simply cannot. Shout-out to all the skilful shearers out there. I love watching them on shearing day, as their muscly arms get oiled up from all the lanolin in the wool. They bring a shearing trailer with a raised section for them to work on: it's almost like a stage and always makes me think of *Magic Mike,* even more so when the music starts playing – mostly country rock. Shearing looks almost like a dance. It smells good, too. Sometimes, I sniff Chris's shirts before they go into the wash because I love the scent of sun cream, sweat and sheep. 'Triple S, the new fragrance from Armani' might not have mass-market appeal but I'd definitely buy it. If you know, you know, and you're my type of person.

The end product – the wool – used to be so valuable, but now it's just a pain in the arse because the price has dropped so low. We spend more paying the shearers to clip the fleeces from the sheep than we're ever paid for them. We sell huge bags of wool – and then get mailed a cheque for a tenner. I'm hopeful, though, that changes might be coming. 'Sustainability' is the word on every-one's lips right now, and the fashion houses are jump-ing on the bandwagon. Plastic and synthetic materials in fabrics are being exposed as damaging to the planet, and surely the answer to these problems should be natural, biodegradable wool.

Whether or not we sell their coats at a profit, there are other reasons why we shear our sheep. One of the main ones is to prevent fly strike. If there's less wool on a sheep's body, flies can't lay their eggs in it. If they do, the maggots will hatch out and start munching their flesh. Nobody deserves that.

One of our ewes was a real Houdini – no matter where we fenced her in, she'd find a way to jump over and make off. On the day we gathered all the ewes for shearing, we had so much buzzing round in our heads that we forgot she was more gazelle than sheep. Before we'd even backed the trailer up to the shearing pen, she'd leapt out and bolted up the valley; her breed, a mixed-breed hill ewe, often sheds its fleece anyway, so we didn't worry about her too much.

It was a bad mistake. A few days later, we found her in the woods. She was in a right old state, kicking at her belly in distress. Chris quickly saw what the problem was. She had fly strike because we hadn't made sure that she was shorn with the others – a big welfare failure on our part. As farmers, it's very difficult to see an animal under your care suffer in any way: you feel such a surge of guilt.

We were also shocked to have fly strike in September – very late in the year when it's more of a summer problem. I posted a video of the poor sheep on Facebook, and before long I was chatting with a handful of farmers from all over the country who were also taken aback to have maggots at this time. A group for maggot sufferers started up – a great example of social media helping with support and advice. Just by typing 'I have that issue too' we all felt less alone.

The miserable feeling is the same when a ewe is suffering from foot-rot – just like the one whose hoof I learned to clip under Chris's instructions – and we've not caught it in time, leading to pus, infection and maggots in the feet. 'If only we'd spotted her sooner . . .' But you'd have a wretched existence on this Earth if you didn't shut down the pity party early on. I've learned to be a vet and a caregiver with eagle eyes to prevent as much illness as possible. But beyond a certain point, there's no more I can do.

The same is true when it comes to the very big picture. Chris and I can be driven to panic and stress by the weather and the changing of the seasons, but that's not under our control. You might reckon a month's drought couldn't do that much damage – dry, patchy grass in the local park, maybe? Your lawn look a bit peaky? When I was a kid, I remember everyone moaning about water shortages when we wanted to fill the paddling pool, and I was thinking how boring adults were. But hit us with a month of no rainfall in May and we're talking major panic stations.

Imagine driving past a field and suddenly seeing a wild-eyed girl in tattered shorts standing in the middle, frantically stabbing holes in a hosepipe. That was me in the glorious May of 2020, when days of blue skies and baking sunshine had wilted the delicious sweet-tasting young grass shoots our new lambs love to eat. A drought can cripple us in weeks, and Chris and I had already banned the subject after 7 p.m. that spring because of the constant worry. Why stoke the flames of despair before bedtime? I had also deleted the weather apps on my phone to rein in my obsessive checking for climatic changes every twenty minutes. (I remember once seeing a TV sketch show poking fun at farmers for never being happy with the weather: too wet, too dry, too hot, too cold – it was never bloody right. And *I'm now that girl.* I am never, *ever* happy.)

Finally, I ended up in that field clutching a hose with handmade holes that was now working (sort of) like a home-made sprinkler system, encouraging the green shoots to grow. If anybody saw me, I probably looked funny. But I was desperate. Sheep die so easily – remember, Death loves them – and all I can do is be on it, every single minute, making sure they don't. But sometimes the odd sheep slips through the net.

I've had to let go. If I hadn't, farming would have broken me. Being with Chris would also have broken me. I can't cure his autoimmune disease. I can't flick my magic wand and stop his joints hurting or prevent him feeling nauseous from exhaustion. I get on with it. It's good to have a passion for the way of life we've chosen. It pushes us to be the best farmers and shepherds we can be, the most vigilant, energetic, strong, the most empathetic. But in the end we're only human, and we accept that.

Sass Queens

'Pigs are drama queens, babe,' Chris warned me. 'When we put the ear tags in, they'll squeal. Especially these pigs.'

'Why especially these?' I asked him.

'Because up to now they've been wild. They've been in the woods foraging for food – basically they've been living their best life out there. Which is great for them, except they've had no handling. So they're not used to people, and now we're trying to get up close and personal.'

In early 2020, Ian asked us for help tagging pigs on his farm over in East Sussex. He's been such a source of support and advice to Chris and me that we were more than happy to go – and his farm's a great place to visit. I was especially looking forward to visiting the collie puppies.

When pigs leave their birthplace, they have to be ear-tagged to ensure they can be traced. The tag goes through the flap of their ear, a bit like being stapled. (The whole process reminds me of having your ears pierced with a needle gun, which stings for a few seconds.) Pigs have very large ears, so you'd think tagging would be quite an easy job – but you'd be wrong. You have to hover the tagging gun extremely carefully and get it in the right position before you start. If you mess up, you've wasted your one chance and you won't be getting a second try. The pig will make sure of that. Once it gets riled, it doesn't want to know.

My job was to stand next to the trailer's lightweight metal gate to make sure it was opened and closed at exactly the right moment to let the boys in or out. But one decided she had other ideas about how to spend her afternoon. She put her nose under the bottom bar of the trailer gate and briskly levered it upwards. I had a few seconds' warning but I didn't react quickly enough: I completely underestimated the strength of a pig and didn't know how sturdy their snouts are. I certainly wasn't expecting the whole gate to come flying up at me – but it wasn't anchored down and the pig lifted it right off its hinges. Out of the blue, it smashed straight into my eye socket and sent me staggering backwards, clutching my face. I really did see stars: the trailer and farmyard were spinning for a moment and the pain was bloody intense.

Chris had been looking at the pig and not at me, which meant he didn't see how hard the gate had hit me. He reacted the way I would have done if he'd had a harmless, slightly ridiculous accident – he burst out laughing. 'Oh, my God!' he cried. 'Emergency! Emergency! Call 999! Tell them to come and sort out her eyebrows!'

Ian, though, was striding towards me. 'Are you okay, Zoë?' he asked.

'Um. Er.' I was finding it quite difficult to speak. My eye socket really, really hurt.

'Chris,' Ian said, 'that gate hit her pretty hard.'

'Let's take a look, Zo!' Chris said to me. I took my hand away and then I saw him wince. 'Oh, shiiiiiit,' he muttered, which spooked me quite a lot because he always plays injuries down.

'Is it bad?' I butted in.

'It's not great, babe.'

I managed to walk to where we'd parked the truck and peered into the wing mirror. I saw blood welling up from a really nasty gash – not a long one, but deep.

'Do you think I need stitches?'

Once we'd finished tagging the pigs, we went to the chemist and bought micropore tape. Ian and Chris stuck it across the cut in very tiny strips and it healed. It was horizontal, luckily, so the scar blended with my right eyebrow. (My eyebrows have always been patchier than

I'd ideally like, so the accident might even have helped thicken this one.) I also knew the damage could have been so much worse: it might have seriously injured my eye. I'd been lucky.

But it could have been avoided entirely if I'd understood better the character of the animals I was dealing with. Since I'd started farming I'd learned so much about my own character. Now I was realizing just how important it was to understand theirs.

* * *

'Why are all your animals so sassy, Zo?' Chris asked me one morning.

'Ha! Like their owner, I guess.' I grinned, as I ducked my head to jump into the truck, not wanting to be late for the vet.

As soon as we'd walked into the barn that morning, the sun barely risen, I knew that Roo, my favourite Pygmy goat and soulmate, wasn't well. My biggest pinch-me moment – when I felt I'd made it in life – was becoming her mum. She's my little pocket rocket, a triplet whose mum didn't give her much milk. I could see she wasn't thriving so I made the decision to take Roo off her mother and rear her myself.

She was probably the cutest thing I'd ever laid my eyes on and Chris used to do his jobs with her in his farming overalls' front pocket, like a kangaroo – hence the name.

She did the tiniest poos, like little golden nuggets, and they made me love her even more. Three times a day we had to milk one of the other goats into a jug to feed her and I once drove forty-five minutes to a goat farm to buy her some extra when the girls were struggling to keep up. I was so worried about her that every night I used to say a little ritual in my head that she wouldn't die.

Roo treated me like her mother – like she had imprinted on me. She went everywhere with me from when she was twenty-four hours old, and screamed for me if I went out of her sight. Even now, although she doesn't look to me for milk any more, she still gives me insane amounts of love, affection and sass. All goats are sassy, but in true Pygmy style, she's super-feisty and her personality is way out of proportion to her size. I'm so into that. Even though she peed and pooed on Indie's bed (twice!), jumped on ours and peed on my pillow, she still can do no wrong in my eyes.

But right now she wasn't standing up on her back legs to say good morning, little hoofs on the lowest gate rung, tail wagging uncontrollably as she heard the truck pull up. She didn't dive face first into the trough to gorge on her favourite snacks. Instead, she was standing in the corner of the pen with the saddest eyes, hunched over in a state of unhappiness that was completely out of character. This was serious, so Chris rang the vet and I fetched Indie's bed from the caravan to put on the front seat of the truck for Roo.

'She's incredibly dehydrated and it's most likely a stomach virus,' said Catherine, our local farm vet. I breathed a sigh of relief. 'We'll hang on to her, if that's okay? I'd like to give her some fluids and keep an eye on her temperature.'

'Anything she needs,' I blurted out. This was Roo, so money didn't come into it. I'd sell a kidney for her. But at least she wasn't seriously ill. I decided that this news called for celebration, so once I'd finished my other errands, I nipped into the posh coffee shop down the road for an iced caramel frappé with an extra espresso shot to drink on the way home. I'd only just pulled into the farm drive – and hadn't even finished the sublime coffee – when my phone flashed up with the vet's number.

My heart skipped a beat. *The vet said Roo was going to be okay. So why's she ringing?*

'Hello?' I answered nervously.

'Hi. Is that Zoë?'

'Um – yes. Is it Roo? Is she—?'

'Oh, yes, it's Roo. You're going to have to pick her up. We've rehydrated her and she's obviously feeling a lot more herself because she's trashing the place. She keeps chewing her IV lines. She's got through four already.'

I clapped my hand to my mouth so the vet's assistant couldn't hear me giggling as I imagined Roo running riot, causing havoc without a thought for the consequences. *That's my girl.*

I drove back, and as I pulled into the vet's small car

park, I could already hear a distinctive, high-pitched *meeeeh!* coming from inside. *It must be loud if it's travelled this far*, I thought, as I jumped out and sped towards the sound. It was indeed Roo, and she was screaming the place down.

'Are you Roo's mum?' asked the lady on the desk.

'Um – yeah.' I gave her my brightest smile, trying to pretend I couldn't hear the bedlam in the room behind me. Then Catherine came out with Roo on a dog lead and hastily handed her over to me. She didn't have to say, 'Thank the Lord you're here to take her,' it was written all over her face.

'Hmm. She's quite a character,' she said, not even trying to hide her relief that we were leaving. 'Shall we put it on the farm account?'

'Do you know what? I'll pay for this myself.' I fumbled for my personal bank card. *Definitely better to pay for Roo's eviction from the vet's because the less Chris knows about this escapade the better.* Roo strutted out to the car, hoofs clip-clopping on the concrete, while I scuttled along beside her, like a parent whose kid had played up at a birthday party and knows they'll never be invited back.

* * *

My original Pygmy goat, Effie – the Farm Cat, as we call her, and the first Pygmy birth I ever saw – has also been a rather unforgettable patient at the vet's. Fully grown

Pygmies are around the height of a small Labrador but with the belly of a pot-bellied pig, a sharp set of horns and a beard that any Shoreditch hipster would envy. Effie is a beautiful brown with a black mohawk zigzagging along her back that rises when she's feeling extra sassy. She was the second of twins and the first arrived quite easily, but when Effie appeared she was still tightly wrapped in her birth sac. I had to break it quickly so that she could breathe. It was very early days and I still wasn't sure what I was doing, so to handle that alone was quite traumatic.

One morning I noticed she was fighting the billy goat continually, not interested in breakfast (unheard of) and vocal to the point of being pretty annoying – all promising signs that she was ready to mate. And we'd even fixed her up with the man of her dreams, a billy goat called Ladd. Ladd was a long-haired, pure-bred Pygmy with horns – we'd searched for months for the perfect guy for Effie and been delighted when we'd found him.

'Eff, you're meant to be shagging Ladd, not fighting him!' I told her, while I was refilling the water trough. Once I'd finished in the barn, I went out to check the group of ewes in the back field.

As I came back down the track to the barn, I could hear the distinctive sound of a billy getting jiggy. Goats are even randier than sheep and they like to shout about it. Someone must have come into season. I could smell it – when billy goats get randy, they wee on their beard, legs and chest to make themselves more attractive to the females. (I can never help cringing a bit, though, at the thought of their piss-saturated beards flopping all over the girls' backs – it really is enough to turn anyone's stomach.) But when I entered the back paddock, I couldn't believe my eyes. Someone was getting jiggy all right, but it was somebody who shouldn't.

We keep the goats apart by size so that no one can go mating where it's going to cause them problems: if a Pygmy female gets in kid with a brick-shithouse-sized goat, like a Boer, it's going to be extremely difficult for her to deliver. (The best way to picture this is to imagine the outcome if a Rottweiler impregnated a miniature poodle.) But Effie had climbed several fences and decided to pay a visit to the big goats' pen. As she seductively swayed her back end in front of his face, Biggie the billy goat was in a frenzy, tongue lolling out of his mouth, wailing with pure frustration. (Type 'goats mating' into YouTube for an eye-opening experience – it really is a sight to behold. The noises, the lip-licking, the beard-flicking . . . I've been to nightclubs in South London in my time and seen worryingly similar scenes.)

Biggie was getting hot and horny while Effie was just standing there as cool as a cucumber, giving him the minimum effort required to get what she wanted (which is pretty standard behaviour for Effie). As I instantly yelled, '*Nooooooo!*' I swear she turned to me and gave me the face that said, 'Yeah – and what?' Pure attitude. I guess she didn't want to be dictated to about who she was going to make kids with, so if she thought Biggie was more her type of baby daddy she went and got him. But it turned out to be the costliest shag of her life. We couldn't take the chance that Biggie might have hit the target, so a few days later I was back at the vet's, holding Effie steady while the vet gave her the goat equivalent of the morning-after pill.

A few months later we did breed from her – with a more suitable boyfriend this time – and she had twins. We got used to seeing the three of them out exploring.

'Have you seen Effie's girls today, babe?' Chris asked, one evening in the spring of 2022.

I thought about it and began to get worried: Effie had been round our feet in the barn earlier on asking for snacks, and one of her two kids had been with her then . . . but I couldn't remember when I'd last seen the three together. As we started searching, a worry was growing in my mind: *Pygmy goats are popular pets. What if she's been stolen?* But then Chris spotted a little clump of brownish hair floating in the pond. It was Effie's missing kid – she'd fallen in and drowned. It was heartbreaking and we felt terribly guilty – the way we always do when something awful happens. But she'd burrowed under *three fences* to get to that pond. How do you keep someone safe when they're as determined as that to do what they want? Goats are wayward, a law unto themselves.

We have many different breeds at our farm and they tend (mostly!) to stick to their own tribes. We've got the Anglo Nubians with their long silky ears and kind faces, really lanky, which makes them look leaner than others, like supermodels. That's where the likeness ends, though, since they're not at all princessy. They're the politest goats in the world: they never bully for food and they're often soppy. They're also super-sensitive to weather and get all upset and mopey when it rains. If they're caught outdoors in a shower, they shriek dramatically and gallop back inside, their ears flying behind them, then have a duvet day.

Next the Pygmies: there's Effie (naturally!) ruling the roost with Roo as her deputy, both of them free rangers who often hop the gate and mingle with the others. Pygmies are very short and stout. They have a huge range of coats, colours, lengths and textures – and all of them come with attitude problems. They butt and fight each other continually and even bite each other's bums if they get really wound up. You'd think with these personality traits they would be very high maintenance, but quite the opposite. In fact, they're as hardy as you like and are rarely unwell, with great feet and strong stomachs. They're larger than life, as long as you keep up their snack intake. Banana skins and raw pasta are their vice. They'd do anything for some penne. Then there are the Boers – the chunky ones, looking like miniature Shetland ponies – and a few cross-breeds.

And, finally, to round off our collection, we have the crème de la crème of the goat world, complete with the hair of Tina Turner and the personality (plus brains) of Phoebe Buffay from *Friends*. The Angoras. Chris knew I'd love them right from the start. Once a hairdresser, always a hairdresser, and I'm a sucker for anything with good hair. It's just as well I am, because some of them have been quite a challenge.

Our very first Angora billy would shag anything – including trying to mount me several times. But at least his desires were straightforward. Next we had Gilbert, whose personality was frankly worrying and just not appealing at all. Although he was a 'wether', meaning he didn't have balls and couldn't sire kids, he'd hang around just over my shoulder and stare, watching whatever I was doing through his curly fringe like some creepy old man. I tried not to read too much into this, but it was quite disturbing. When two of my Pygmies were leaving to go to a new home, he developed a massive crush on the woman who was taking them, and followed her around obsessively on all her visits to the farm. Gilbert's story has a happy ending: eventually he was rehomed with a woman named Suzanne who got along with him far better than I ever could. She told me he joins in whenever she has friends round to dinner and that everybody loves him – his social skills must have improved.

Then we have the superstar, Tina. She's the complete opposite to Gilbert, a loner and an oddball who goes her own way, floating between the goat tribes and never truly fitting in, but in no way bothered about it. Her coat is sensational, with tight white ringlets, enough to give us all hair envy. We shear her every couple of months because her curls can easily get matted with debris or infested with lice, but she's so wild and feisty that I struggle to trim her. I may have been a professional hairdresser but she's ended up with a few dodgy haircuts. When Chris was putting up the electric fence to keep the goats out of our landlady's garden, Tina stood absolutely silent behind him the entire time. It wasn't until the job was done that he realized he'd fenced her out, not in.

She didn't get pregnant the first year she was with us because she just didn't want to know. We decided she was shy and needed a bit longer before she was ready to date. When we tried a second time, she seemed up for it, coming into heat and sniffing round the billy. Then we tried to scan her and we couldn't – her coat was too fluffy to find a patch of skin for the ultrasound. We were pretty sure she must be in kid, though, so we decided to wait and see. But she wasn't.

'That's a weird goat, Zo,' Chris said thoughtfully.

In her third year on the farm we tried her again with the billy, but this time we sheared a little patch on her belly to make it easier for her scan. Malcolm, our scanner, had been working a long day and there were only two goats left for him to check by the time he got to Tina. This time round he managed to get her scanning process started, but she was so gassy he couldn't get a reading. The blurry images on the screen might have been embryo kids but then again, they might have been spectacular farts.

'I'm really sorry,' Malcolm kept saying. 'Time will tell!'

Tina had a kid in July 2022, a healthy male Pygora, the

first ever born on the farm. They really are the cutest goat kids ever. But even though she's a mum now, she's still her own woman: she's never going to follow the herd.

* * *

'The truck won't go down there, babe. We're never gonna manage it in a million years!'

'That's why no one else wanted to graze it, Zo. This is the access.'

It was May 2022 and Chris and I were out on a new job – a conservation-grazing gig, using sheep to improve the habitat. (Eat and poo, guys. Eat and poo.) Perhaps it has orchids or bellflowers growing there, or it's a night-ingales' nesting site. Ten sheep might go out in a field for six weeks, then leave so that the orchids can flower.

Conservation land often hasn't been looked after too well and is in a poorer state, which usually means farmers or graziers aren't desperate to take it on. Poorer land also means that we have to be careful about which animals can graze there: we put Highland cattle or Shorthorns, for example, onto ground where others would struggle. This is when it helps to keep such an eclectic mix of breeds as we do. Sometimes nibbling the top of the grass shoots that sheep enjoy is enough to keep the ground in good nick but it's a constant balancing act: you can overgraze and deplete the ground. Managing all our different plots can get complicated, but we still love being a part of these things: it's an adventure, and we're playing a role in the good stewardship of the countryside.

This time we'd been paid to put ten sheep on a small piece of an SSSI, a Site of Special Scientific Interest, deep in a wood (but fortunately with water piped in to fill the troughs) and we'd decided that the Soays and Hebrideans – both petite breeds, horned and wild – were our best bet for the location. The owner had assured us that our trailer and truck would definitely fit so it would be easy to get the sheep down there. Okay – except that when we turned up with the first five girls, the only access turned out to be a pathway about a metre wide. There was no way any vehicle would get through, and we'd have to do this job on foot. Now we could see why they were paying for it to be grazed.

We stood and stared down the shady path beneath the trees. Then I had a brainwave, 'Wait a minute. I've got Indie's harness and lead – what d'ya reckon?'

Chris cracked up laughing. 'What – put the lead on the sheep? We've lost the plot!'

'Let's just think about this,' I said to him. 'We've got baling twine in the boot. Get on YouTube and see if there's instructions on how to make a sheep halter.'

We tried to contain our giggles while Chris cut lengths of twine with his knife and we attempted to fashion something sturdy enough to control a Soay sheep. They're pretty much untameable – except that now we were gearing up to walk them a mile through woodland, knowing full well that if they got away, we'd never see them again. All we'd be left with would be blurred photos of them on local Facebook groups taken by dog-walkers.

'What happens if there are dogs on this path?' I asked Chris.

He rolled his eyes. 'Let's just hope there aren't, eh?'

He climbed out of the trailer with the first sheep he'd picked for this adventure, a black Hebridean. I took a deep breath and followed with one of the Soays. She was half the size of his but she must have had her Weetabix that morning because she flew out of the trailer like a bat out of hell, dragging me after her, my sunglasses shooting off my head. This pretty much set the tone for the rest of the morning. Chris's girl was great – a bit of stopping and starting, some sniffing and wees, but she trotted alongside him most of the way without too much bother. I brought up the rear with my stroppier customer: she struggled and resisted every step until I was either pulling her along by her horns or carrying her in my arms. She must have weighed 15 kilos and each time I had to lift her, she wriggled and writhed furiously. I was constantly bracing myself for a horn to the nose, or worse.

'She's a proper princess! Imagine getting carried all the way to her lush grass and breathtaking, panoramic views!' I yelled to Chris from ten metres behind him, arms throbbing and beads of sweat running down my back.

I heard him laugh. 'My girl's a dreamboat, babe! Wanna

swap?' I absolutely did want to swap, but I'm also very stubborn and there was no way I was admitting that I was struggling. Mind you, my scarlet face and growing sweat patches probably gave it away, along with my continual muttered swear words and demands of 'Are you serious?' to the sheep.

Chris and I did two walks along the path together in the end. He did the last by himself while I recovered, smeared from head to toe in shit, sweat and lanolin and feeling totally wiped out. 'Only five more sheep tomorrow, babe! But how will we ever get them out?' I asked, when he got back.

He just laughed. 'That's a problem for another day!'

* * *

'Bunch o' hippies!' Chris exclaimed as our Highland cattle emerged from the bushes. 'Gonna have to give them fringe trims soon so they can see where they're going.'

They'd arrived a few months earlier and moved onto the chalk Downs, grazing the steep, rough banks, looking perfectly at home and just like a picture postcard. There was Goldie Horn and Una: Goldie the most beautiful sun-kissed yellow (a Wella 9.3 colour swatch, for sure), and Una a vivid strawberry blonde. They were like two woolly mammoths: as they ran towards us, we could almost feel the ground thudding under their weight. Then there was Barbie, a smaller female with bright golden hair, her horns just starting to grow so they looked like little devil spikes poking through the shimmering tresses. The three could have been an advert for shampoo, tossing their locks in the sun.

'Peace out, man,' Chris said to them, in a thick Californian accent as he fed Una a bread roll. Their personalities are so calm and they almost move in slow motion sometimes, so much so that we often joke they've been on the wacky baccy. I swear all they're missing are daisy-chain crowns and they could be hanging out at Glastonbury Festival or celebrating a solstice at Stonehenge. *You just work it, girls. Do your thing.*

The odd one out was Henny, a Hereford female I've had since she was a week old. She's red and white with a short sticky-up fringe, wonky devil horns and eyes that point in different directions – one looking at you and one that looks at the person next to you.

'Hello, darlin'!' I said, as she let me scratch her head and I pulled a sticky burr out of her fringe. 'We can't have you being led astray by these waywards.'

But it was too late. Henny was only twelve weeks old when she took it upon herself to live out with the Highlands – that's quite young to be leaving the barn. Before then, she'd been with the other calves in the shed. It was January and temperatures were getting down to zero at night, so ideally they'd all be tucked in deep straw up to their bellies. We put netting around the open gaps in the barn walls to try to block the icy draughts, or the bitter wind sweeps straight through the barn during the early months of the year.

But Henny wanted to hang with the gang and kept heading out towards the Downs. Three times we walked her back into the cosy barn at nightfall, once in the driving rain and once during a blizzard at minus two. But next morning when I went out lookering in my ski suit and sheepskin hat, vision impaired by the snowstorm, there she was again under the bare trees, sheltering with the hippies. 'Henny,' I said, 'you're an absolute nutter. That's two fences she's hopped over!' I told Chris, as we tried to decide if there was any point in trying to keep her where she was supposed to be. 'She knows what she wants, eh?'

Chris grinned. 'Another of your defiant, headstrong animals. I guess she's staying out there, then, Zo.'

* * *

By the spring of 2021, Goldie Horn was in calf to Mr Biggles. Everything seemed to be progressing well and she'd started bagging up in preparation for the birth. She was on the Downs, grazing in a protected area where a rare orchid grows, and we were doing regular checks on her. But early one warm, bright morning, Chris found she'd delivered in the night and her premature calf was lying dead on the ground. I was shocked, but also relieved that I hadn't found it: I'd have been nervous that Goldie might behave aggressively, with all those birth hormones circulating and confused maternal instincts over the calf she'd lost. Not to mention that it would have been difficult for me to lift the body on my own.

Chris noticed that Goldie hadn't yet expelled the placenta (also known as the afterbirth: the thick pad of tissue that connects the umbilical cord to the uterine wall). Every birth must be followed by the placenta coming away from the mother's body: retention can cause serious infection. The problem is easier to deal with in sheep than in cattle: for a ewe, an injection can help, or the placenta can be gently pulled free. It's much harder to intervene like this with a cow.

Chris bribed Goldie with some bread and injected her rump to protect her against infection. Then he thought he'd give her some more time: the birth was fairly recent and premature, after all, and when a delivery happens early, things don't always go smoothly. He went back the next day, expecting to see the placenta half delivered and hanging out of her. But there was nothing. By now she seemed to be recovering well. It's quite normal for cows to eat their placentas so he guessed that was what she'd done.

Two days later, Goldie died. We found her body on the Downs, an enormous hulk, woolly-mammoth-sized, somehow bigger as she lay there motionless. She hadn't expelled the placenta after all. Toxic shock had killed her. We felt horrible guilt, but the more we went over it, the more we realized there wasn't much we could have done.

If we'd managed to get her into the trailer (quite an 'if' to start with) and then (even bigger 'if') we'd been able to get her into a halter or handling system, it would still have been hard to intervene medically. Her calf had been born so prematurely that the natural process of expelling the placenta just hadn't worked.

Even so, we felt dreadful. We'd given Goldie a name. Her passport gave her date of birth as 2015 so she was only six, and we'd expected her to be with us for many years to come. Cattle can live for up to twenty years and her loss shook us deeply. This wild, graceful Highland breed, so conscious of the vast sweep of their horns, able to turn their heads just one inch left or right to clear their way, had truly captivated us – but could we really manage to care for them?

The universe came to our rescue. The following morning, we discovered that one of our heifers, which we'd known was in calf when we acquired her, had calved during the night. We'd been so down and disheartened, and here was the gift of new life. We experience the best and the worst that Nature can do. She can be bloody brutal, no doubt about it, but she can also bestow the gift of life when you least expect it. It's a lesson I relearn every time.

* * *

I'll never forget the arrival of Bambi. As our other new calves – all Friesians and Holsteins – walked off the trailer,

I could see that Chris was grinning. And when I saw who was hiding at the back, I realized why.

'That's your Christmas present, Zo!' he said. She was a gorgeous Jersey calf with a caramel-coloured coat flecked with white, and she'd got her name because she looked more like a fawn, delicate and leggy with wide brown eyes and sweeping film-star lashes. Who wants an iPad as a gift when they can have a new pet cow?

'But no one ever sells the girls. D'you think there's something wrong with her?' I asked him. A young female would definitely be kept for breeding by most farmers. We never found out for sure. Perhaps her mother died and wherever she came from was reluctant to rear her on the bottle, or maybe her mother had struggled to provide enough milk for her: having a 'bad bag' can be hereditary and the previous farmer might have hesitated to keep a female calf perhaps with the same problem. But I was delighted to have Bambi. She was tentative, gentle and such an appealing character.

We tag our calves when they're very young simply because of their strength (although the law also backs this up). They grow so fast and get so powerful that if you wait, you'll have problems. If a calf makes a noise or resists, its mother will intervene, and cows can kill you. There's a serious risk of the farmer or the animal being injured. And when farm animals clash with each other, there can also be real damage done.

We winter our cattle in the valley, where the ground

maintains them really well, but it's difficult for us to get access down there, especially when it's wet or if it snows. We don't want to get vehicles stuck or to chew up the land, so we have to take their hay bales and supplies of waste vegetables and brewer's grains on foot. (Brewer's grains are a by-product of the brewing industry and we are fortunate enough to have a brewery just down the road that supplies them for free: all we have to do is pick the stuff up. It's malt so it smells like pubs and looks like porridge, and our cows do well on it.)

Keeping cattle in the valley creates other problems too: it's alongside a big dog-walking route, which can cause misunderstandings. Newborn animals are unsteady on their feet and need time to learn to walk. Sometimes anxious Facebook posts and even phone calls start pouring in: 'You've got a calf in one of your fields that's lame!'

Once she got stronger, Bambi went out there, and that was where she met Blue. Blue was a Belgian Blue cross that had been sickly and on special-needs care since she was born. She had come pretty close to dying more than once. I'd worked hard with her medication and made sure she was always covered with straw at night to keep her really warm. One thing I noticed was the way she held her head – it was never quite straight and always on the slant. I wondered if she'd had some kind of neurological infection that had left her with balance issues.

Cows operate very much as a herd. Like elephants, they tend to have a matriarch in charge and a strong hierarchy going on – at least, in our small herd they always do. I've never seen full-on punch-ups between them but when there's food up for grabs you can soon tell who's bottom of the pack because they'll be left with the crumbs once everyone else has had enough. By the time Bambi (and a few others) was weaned and went out into the field, Blue and her cronies were in charge. If Bambi wanted their respect, she'd have to earn it. It's the sort of situation that immediately puts me on edge.

We pay a lot of attention to our girls and I was keeping a special eye on Bambi. That was why I spotted straight away that she'd been hurt. She'd been in the field for a few months and I thought they'd all accepted one another. But then I noticed that her eye socket was red and badly swollen, with clouds of flies buzzing round it and dried bloody tears staining her face. Still, she was such a trouper that she didn't seem that bothered by her injury. Cows are resilient, and in a large herd it's possible for injuries like this to be missed. That's not at all the case with sheep: I swear that a sheep with a sore eye would have collapsed straight away and would most likely be trying its best to die from it.

Bambi needed antibiotics, but treating sick cattle is very different from treating sick sheep. They're so much larger and stronger. We'd never had a cow of this size that needed antibiotics before, and at this stage of our farming career, we didn't have the equipment we needed to hold Bambi in position so that she could have her injections. Eventually we managed to jab her with anti-biotics by using snacks as bribes or having Chris ride her, like a bucking bronco. After three wild days of treatment, the swelling and soreness were much less. Now that her wound was clean, we could see just how serious it was.

'Jesus, Chris!' I said. 'Something's poked her eye out!' All that was left in the socket was a sticky, pulpy mess. We deliberated over what might have happened. Could a crow have pecked it out? That happens to sheep, but only when they're down and lying still. Bambi was as right as rain. After much deliberating and peering at the injury, we decided that it had most likely been caused by a horn.

We tend to dehorn the dairy calves we rear. First, they sell better in the market if they aren't horned, but in the long term it's safer when you're working with a large powerful animal if they don't have a weapon to kebab you with. We'd cauterized and popped out the horn buds on most of the calves when they were small, but there'd been one that was too weak and poorly to go through the procedure (which involves numbing the area) at the time – and that had been Blue. She had started to sport some rather pointy, devilish horns.

'D'you reckon she had Bambi's eye out with those?' I asked Chris, as we watched them hoovering up some fodder beet. Blue was certainly demonstrating that she knew exactly where her horns were and was taking pleasure in using them. We could see that all the other cows were giving her a very wide and careful berth.

'Wouldn't put it past her,' Chris replied. But there was no way to know for sure. Bambi's injury had fully healed and she was definitely channelling her inner pirate: all she needed was the eyepatch. Whatever had happened, the field seemed calm again.

Many farms might not have let a one-eyed cow breed in case she had problems as a mother: she might accidentally lie on her calf, or tread on it, or hurt it in some other way. We didn't mind so much because we thought of Bambi as a pet, and in the end, she saw Mr Biggles the Hereford bull. He was an incredible unit who could crush you without even trying: I've never seen a brisket as wobbly as his. As we have such a small herd of only fifteen or so adult cows at a time, it means we can watch what's happening very closely, so we weren't worried about her disability. It was late November when Bambi calved (with a bit of assistance from Chris), and we were certain, as she licked and fussed over the tiny newborn, that she was going to be a fabulous mother. We named the female calf Bambino and it became clear very quickly that the lusciously rich and creamy Jersey milk Bambi produced was doing wonders. She grew at such a rate that she was quickly catching up with the others born three weeks before her.

* * *

I love how we can go with the flow when it comes to our animals. If someone is a character, or has prima-donna tendencies, we can cope with it. If we want to keep a goat around just because we like him, no problem. If we fancy taking a chance on breeding from a charismatic Curly Sue (like Tina, who really is a seriously weird goat), sure, no stress. And if someone's a queen of total sass, we can say, 'Okay,' just let them do their thing and have a chance to hang out with us – just like Henny, Goldie Horn, Una, Roo, Effie and Bambi. These guys make their own rules.

The Tapeworm Takes One for the Team

'Do you mind if I get the other doctors in here? I'm sure they'd like to see this.'

I've sat in a few medical surgeries, but never one where the staff are googling my condition in front of me. My GP rang both of her partners and everyone trooped into her consulting room looking excited. Orf, or 'scabby mouth', as it's called among sheep farmers, spreads like wildfire in sheep, starting on the mouths and noses of lambs when they're feeding, then infecting their mothers' teats. Humans can catch it from them, and from cattle too, and it causes flaky sores and looks very grim and skanky. My orf started as a tiny itchy bump on my finger and I knew straight away what it was because so many people had warned me about it.

I still wear rings as a farmer, but nowadays I make sure that all of them fit flat to my fingers. In the early days, I had a lovely onyx ring with jagged edges and it had slightly nicked my hand. I didn't even notice – but orf spreads through broken skin and a few days later that little raised bump appeared. It grew bigger and bigger and I started to feel tired, the way you do when your body's fighting off an infection. I tried treating it with cold-sore cream, then googled what to do and had a go with crushed rock salt and tight bandages. Eventually, I had to accept that orf is a virus and not much really works. That was why I went to my GP, which turned out to be a completely wasted trip where treatment was concerned, although everyone at the surgery wanted to look. I felt like something in a zoo. They didn't have much to suggest, except that if it started spreading along my arm or my temperature went up, it might be sepsis and that could be more serious. Then they came close to asking for a selfie with the weird sheep girl.

The orf went away over the next few months, but it was miserably itchy and the only thing that helped was sitting in cold baths. There must be a lord above, though, because at least it never spread to my face. Nowadays I always wear gloves when I'm working with lambs, even if there's no orf in sight. It could always be lurking. I absolutely hate the idea of being ill.

My problem with sickness is actually more serious than that. An overwhelming, all-consuming phobia of being unwell or throwing up. It's totally a control issue. When you feel that hot fuzzy feeling creeping over you, your mouth waters uncontrollably, and your insides start to contract – you just know what's going to happen next. You have no control and that's what freaks me out. I've lost count of the times I've tried to hold in the sick, breathed through the panic, pursed my lips so incredibly tightly that no vomit could exit. But it always finds a way out (note to self: it usually makes even more mess when you try to contain it). For some people, that feeling of knowing it's coming but having no control of your bodily functions is scary and emotionally scarring. That's the case with me.

For a long time, I couldn't understand why this was. There'd been no awful dramas in my childhood, to my knowledge, so how had I become, in this respect at least, a bit messed up? Eventually I had some therapy to help me deal with it, and during my sessions I discovered a few situations in my past that had left me terrified of sickness. There was the time that my sister projectile-vomited all over the back of our car – and me. We were on a motorway at the time, so no one could escape. I once trashed a new stair carpet by throwing up all over it, top step to bottom, and even though my mum was really kind and not angry at all, I could tell that what I'd done was a bit of a disaster. A boy at my junior school was sick suddenly in assembly one day, and that had freaked me out. I'd forgotten all those incidents until I did the therapy, but a dread of losing control like that had taken hold in my childhood and then just grew up with me. I lost sight of the cause and was left with the frightening effect: a sickness phobia that hindered me for the best part of twenty years and nearly derailed my first date with Chris back in Stoke Newington.

This problem caused me endless wretched worry and led me to boycott certain foods. I had an eating blacklist, which kept changing all the time. I'd find out that a client's cousin's husband said he'd got food poisoning from the restaurant down the road . . . so on to the list it went, and I'd avoid it like the plague. My levels of anxiety ebbed and flowed. There were times when I obsessed over use-by dates or would eat only 'safe foods' – ones I didn't think were high risk for food poisoning. At other times, I could allow myself to eat at certain restaurants as long as I'd checked the menu first and the food-hygiene rating. I mean, everyone checks that kind of stuff three times before they go out, don't they?

All this anxiety made going on holiday a bit complicated. I'd absolutely dread it. I could fill this whole chapter with the things I'd panic about: being in the airport and getting trapped by a flight delay once I'd gone through security, being trapped on a plane marinating in everyone else's germs for six hours, not being able to get to a toilet when the seatbelt sign was on, someone else not getting to a toilet when the seatbelt sign was on, getting sick from ice in a gin and tonic. It was exhausting and built up into a serious phobia of flying. My GP prescribed diazepam for this, and that seemed to work okay although, of course, it didn't help with the underlying issues.

When I was twenty-one, I went to Thailand with my ex-boyfriend and a group of about twenty others for his sister's wedding. Every client and colleague was green-eyed with envy – it was the most miserable time of the year in cold, rainy London and I was escaping to the sun. Except I didn't look at it like that. All I could think about was how everyone gets sick in Asia and I was bound to be struck down with salmonella on day one and get stranded thousands of miles from home, projectiling from both ends every five minutes. I was sick with worry upon worry upon worry. I don't think I had more than three minutes the entire holiday where my mind wasn't racing, super-sensitive to the slightest cough, or burp, or anything that sounded or felt like 'I don't feel well.' I barely slept or ate for the whole two weeks we were there and I didn't poo once. My boyfriend had no idea what was going on: he just thought I was a miserable cow and didn't realize I was having a breakdown. So this fortnight in paradise also turned out to be the last straw for a relationship that was shaky already. It just goes to show that things aren't always as they seem.

I never voiced any of these fears until I was with Chris. It felt impossible to tell anyone, so I walked around with this overpowering secret. But right at the start of our relationship, when his autoimmune disease first started, he was the most vulnerable he had ever been and that made it possible for me to be vulnerable too. I'd seen his very first panic attack in Stoke Newington on the day we'd intended to go to the zoo, and he knew I understood. It was a green light for me to be honest, so I told him and he listened. Without realizing it, he allowed me to be truly myself.

* * *

You might be wondering, with all this going on, how I cope with being close to the animals. Especially sheep, which, if they can't quite manage to die for kicks, will settle for being seriously ill. Well, first of all – *sheep can't be sick*. They cannot physically vomit. I felt fairly safe with them. (Okay, there are a few zoological diseases that they can transmit to humans but at least they aren't airborne.) But, second, it hasn't been easy and I've really had to work on my issues.

The main illnesses to watch out for on farms are worms, E. coli, salmonella, campy (campylobacteriosis), crypto (cryptosporidiosis), coxi (coccidiosis) and toxo (toxoplasmosis). Any one of those can see you pinned to the toilet for a week or more and, to start with, just the thought of it had me in hot sweats. I vividly remember the first time I was faced with the prospect of catching a bug from farm animals. It was early spring and freezing cold, I was still working at the salon and when I arrived at Chris's house for the night, three lifeless-looking hypothermic lambs were lying on a blanket in the sitting room.

Instantly I had butterflies. *Shit*, I thought. *I'm gonna have to hold one of those.* Then Chris's mum said, 'There was another but it died of E. coli. We think these might have it too' – and that was it. Just the words 'E. coli' sent me spiralling down a rabbit hole of imaginary bellyaches and convincing myself I'd catch it from particles in the air. I freaked out. I had to get out of there.

One of the lifeless lambs turned out to be Penelope, still in our flock today. She didn't stand for days and was literally a pincushion from the amount of times she had to be injected with various medicines and vitamins. That's why we called her Penny – she runs on penicillin. It wasn't until she was well (and I knew I couldn't get sick from her) that I finally allowed us to bond.

The next time I came across E. coli was a serious outbreak in the pet pen. It was a bitter, soaking spring and our lambs were being born outdoors. They weren't getting up straight away in all the rain and wind, so they weren't getting their colostrum quickly enough and quite a few were going down with exposure. Eventually I had so many frail lambs in the barn that I had to label them and set up a whiteboard to record all the reasons why they were there and their medicines.

Then came the outbreak. It happened because we'd given the pregnant ewes free rein of all the fields so they'd lambed in different places, leaving afterbirth and poo all around. They lay down and got dirt on their udders. When their lambs were born – with no antibodies yet – they went straight on the teat and the result was E. coli. We learned from our mistake, and nowadays we always make sure to move the lambers about and keep some clean ground.

E. coli is also called 'watery mouth' and leads to dehydration, collapse and often death. It's easy to identify by the greenish saliva that's dripping around the animal's mouth and chin. My treatment plan begins as follows: warm them up on a bed of fluffy straw with the big red heat lamp on them. Next an antibiotic: I use a small needle to jab a millilitre into their rump muscle. As soon as the lamb is warm enough, it will hopefully hold its head up, and that's when I give them kaolin clay (to detox the gut) and warm water (which hydrates them). Quite soon they should poo, but if they don't I give them an enema: I mix washing-up liquid with warm water and put the tube up their bum. Once it runs clear, you know you've got a clean passage. Then as soon as they're well enough, it's on to colostrum or milk and a vitamin injection. In five or six hours, you can tell what the outcome's going to be: they either turn around quite quickly and start getting to their feet, or they're dead. Although not in every case: I had one lamb that didn't try to stand for four days. We called him Sick Note and Chris thought he wasn't going to make it and was suffering too much, but by day two he was drinking from a bottle. Even though he was still very weak, I thought an effort like that should get Sick Note the benefit of the doubt and I kept on trying. When Chris got back from market on day four, he was up on his feet and drinking unassisted.

The best thing about his recovery was that I'd done it by myself. I'd researched the best approaches, and the advice about kaolin clay came from a Facebook group I'd joined. My own learning had formed my armoury against this outbreak of disease. It was a huge confidence booster.

* * *

In our first ever flock of sheep – those thirty-two Suffolk Mules – we had a scrawny old lady we called Doris. When you first sign on to a farming veterinary practice, the vet comes to do a flock health test before they'll take you, and straight away she said she was worried about Doris. She thought she might have Johne's disease, which is also known as paratuberculosis.

Johne's is a very serious muscle-wasting condition and a sheep that has it ends up as skin and bone with a very poor fleece. Their ears droop and they look drawn and depressed, with their bones jutting out. Johne's can spread quickly, and is transmitted from one to another in their poo, so any infected animal must immediately be destroyed. If it had swept through our new flock, we would have had to kill the whole lot – a total disaster, which would have prevented us from going any further. It was an early lesson in the chances we were taking as we started out in farming, and just how precarious our way of life can be.

Our vet understood why we were worried and the problem was dealt with very quickly. But there have been times when she's had to give horrendous news to others. TB in cattle is the one all farmers fear: regular testing is required by law but discovering a positive case in a herd ('getting a reactor') can mean the end of a business and the livelihood of a whole family. It's a black cloud of anxiety that hangs constantly above a farmer's head. The public tends not to sympathize – remember the perception that lots of us are rich – and also there's a view that we see our animals only as a business. But farmers have relationships with their cows that go back years – they know the girls by name and feel really connected to them. Cows are individuals, smart, switched on and full of personality in a way that's just not true of sheep, and having to destroy them is heartbreaking. We only have to test ours for TB every four years, but in some areas it's required every six months.

Then we had yet another scare. In spring 2022, one

of Chris's goats developed lesions on her face and we thought she might have CLA – caseous lymphadenitis, also known in sheep as 'thin ewe syndrome', which pretty much tells you what it does. It causes abscesses in the lymph nodes and internal organs. It's incurable and super-contagious. We were very worried waiting for her blood-test result, and although it turned out she didn't have it, it reminded us – not that we need reminding – of how unexpectedly our fortunes could turn.

* * *

When animal sickness endangers humans, it makes headline news. I was also learning more about the scary history of disease control in farming. Back when Chris was a little boy, deadstock didn't have to be taken away and disposed of in the way the law now requires. Next time the knacker man (the 'deadman') came around, I plucked up the courage to ask him what had happened and why the rules were changed.

'The BSE crisis,' he told me grimly. 'Mad cow disease, back in the nineties. It was lots of work for me – I've never been so busy – but everyone I met was in despair. It was political, too. People didn't sympathize. They thought the farmers were to blame. It left a lot of trauma.'

After BSE, the law was changed and stricter rules were brought in about burying deadstock. Before the 1990s you could do this in a pit on your own land but now,

because of the fear that infected carcasses could con-
taminate the soil or the waterways, you have to pay for
them to be taken away. There were new rules for abattoirs as well, and the brains and spinal cords have to be
destroyed over a specific age, and vets at abattoirs look
carefully to make sure the slaughtered animal was healthy.
The first time I saw slashes in livers or hearts, I thought
our abattoir must employ a really sloppy butcher, but it
was part of a super-careful system of checks to protect
human health. Regulations for transporting livestock are
also very strict and everything that goes on at the markets
is closely monitored.

In 2001 came foot-and-mouth disease. I vaguely
remember watching TV and seeing horrendous images
of flaming pyres of cattle that had had to be destroyed to
stop its spread. I was a child and didn't really understand
what was happening, but I think there was sympathy for
farmers then. People understood that they were victims
of the devastating spread of the disease.

We're always at the mercy of something: of the
weather, of infection, negative reporting in the media,
fluctuating prices in the market. Currently, in 2022, the
price of diesel and red diesel – that's the fuel that can be
used only for farm equipment – is rising very quickly.
This means that the hay-baling machine will cost more
to run, which makes the hay more expensive and raises
the cost of feeding our animals. That's just one example
of the complex web of cause and effect we constantly

have to navigate. We do all we can to control the spread of disease on the farm. We watch our animals like hawks, we learn as much as we can about how to keep them healthy and we treat them as fast as we can if they get sick. But we can never feel secure – and that's just the way it is.

* * *

I wasn't feeling unwell, but in the summer of 2019, I noticed that although I'd been eating loads I was still losing weight. My clothes had started hanging off me, and I usually weigh the same no matter what, so this was weird. But perhaps I'd just been extra-active and used up more energy than usual. There was maybe the odd gripe in my belly, but these days I'm less anxious when I feel something like that. Then one day I went to the loo, and when I wiped, I saw a tapeworm.

I sat there and stared. Then I started shaking. There was no question at all that this was what it was: I'd seen tapeworms before in lambs and sheep. The worm was pale, about two inches long, and looked a bit like a piece of tagliatelle or a long, flat noodle. Very carefully, I pulled it apart and examined it. I had no idea how I'd been infected. Just automatically I flushed it away (it occurred to me afterwards that it would have been more sensible to keep hold of it), then walked out of the bathroom and sat down cross-legged on the bed in total shock. My heart was hammering so fast that I'm surprised Chris couldn't see it exploding out of my chest. Some people go pale when they panic, but not me. I go bright red. Getting more and more scarlet by the minute, I mumbled, 'Something bad happened in there.'

'Babe?' Chris said. 'What happened, babe?'

'Um. So. Right. Please don't not fancy me, but I think I just pooed out a tapeworm.'

'Are you sure?'

'Yes, Chris! I'm sure! We both know what they look like.'

But then, in the back of my mind, a little thought pinged up. *Oh, my God. Am I imagining this? Could it be a part of my sickness phobia? Is it a new symptom, maybe?* I took a deep breath. *No. No way. I know what it was. I examined it.*

I rang my GP, who was incredibly dubious. She insisted that a tapeworm was very unlikely to be what I had seen: people in the UK don't get them, she said, and even if somebody did, to expel one is really, really rare. *But I know what I saw.*

In the end she agreed that I should bring a sample of my poo to the surgery. I arrived with one in a Tupperware container that I normally use to store Victoria sponge, but then I noticed that all the other samples in the basket were in special little poo pots with labels. No one had given me one of those, so mine would be the only anonymous poo. I was in a huge flap by now and desperate to escape so I left my sample and scarpered.

But when I got back to the van I sat there thinking, *Oh, God, I should have labelled the pot. I have to go back in and ask them for a label. Are they going to let me do that?* In the end they told me they'd label it themselves.

I had to wait a week, and then I was notified by text. It was a negative result: there were 'no infestations' so apparently I hadn't had a worm. I was still completely certain that I had, but there didn't seem a lot I could do, apart from try not to worry about it. Another fortnight went by, and then the phone rang. It was Mum.

'You've got a letter from the NHS, Zobes,' she said. 'They must think this is still your home address. D'you want me to read it?'

'Sure.'

I heard the envelope rustling, followed by a weird little silence, and then Mum just said, 'Oh!'

My stomach dropped. 'Mum? What is it?'

'Hmm. Okay. So, it's from Public Health England.'

'What? Oh, my God. Why?'

'It says you have a notifiable disease. Umm . . . it's called STEC. Have you ever heard of that?'

'Nope.'

'Er . . . It says here it's a form of E. coli.'

I went straight online, and started learning all I could. STEC lives in the digestive tracts of cattle. It's produced by the Shiga toxin, and symptoms include severe stomach cramps, bloody diarrhoea and vomiting. It was just about the most disturbing, frightening illness I could ever think of having. I kept researching, and by 2 a.m. the following morning, I'd burrowed my way into a deep, dark corner of the internet. That was where I discovered something else. I found a case – a real live case – where someone had a tapeworm and it actually died of STEC. This is definitely possible.

In my half-awake state, I blearily wondered what on earth had just happened. Perhaps I'd been protected from illness by my unexpected passenger. Instead of making me ill, what if my STEC had killed it and that's why I was okay? There's no way to be sure. But just in case that's right, I'd like to take the opportunity to say a very big thank-you. I think that tapeworm might have taken one for the team.

Slaughter

'Hey,' said Chris, 'could I please get a grilled chicken pitta, mate, medium spice and peri-peri fries?'

Shit. Why haven't I told him I'm a veggie yet? But standing in the queue at a famous chicken restaurant definitely wasn't the best time to mention it. A farmer's son and a vegetarian: this was going to be quite the romance.

Until I met Chris, I chose not to eat meat. There were quite a few reasons for this, and one of them – of course – was my long-term phobia of sickness. Cheap meat is a food-poisoning risk and high-quality products are expensive, so I felt much safer eating Quorn. Anyway, I had better things to spend my money on, like daiquiris and make-up. My two favourite dinners (when I actually ate dinner) were spinach and ricotta ravioli with butter and basil, and couscous with roasted veg and feta cheese.

I found out very early in our relationship that our dietary habits couldn't have been more different. Chris was a carnivore. Not only that, but the gym was his oasis, his escape from the pressures of running a small business. His body was his temple and he even kept an eye on his carbohydrate and fat intakes. Meanwhile my snacks consisted of cinnamon buns from Gail's and the odd bruised banana. He spent his evenings rustling up the next day's healthy menu and you could have fed the five thousand with one of his packed lunches: bowls of rice, broccoli and tuna fit for a weekend barbecue, along with (probably one of the only times I questioned if we were really meant to be together) turkey meatballs. These really didn't look appealing: grey mounds of dense, dry, tasteless meat that would have encouraged anyone to carry on without the animal products. Still, the way he was eating was obviously doing him some good, and the first time I saw him take his top off was a moment. The guy was an Adonis and alongside all this well-honed muscle, I felt like a malnourished waif living off fags and thin air.

A month into our courtship, Chris roasted a leg of lamb laced with rosemary and garlic that was tempting even for me. I had to endure the stunning smell filling the house for eight hours. When I sat down I stubbornly ate only the vegetables and roast potatoes. But I couldn't shake the thought of that meat being left over, so I snuck down to the kitchen later on for just a little taste. And one thing led to another.

Nowadays, I can't help but think about this odd fact when it comes to eating meat: while most of the British population are lifelong meat eaters, I also know from conversations as a farmer that quite a lot of them are grossed out and disgusted at the thought that what's on their dinner plate was once a living, breathing creature. The idea of meat once being flesh is enough to tip them over the edge – the blood, the bones, and God forbid they spot anything that looks like a body part, like trotters, for example.

Our brains don't like to link the flesh and bone on the neatly labelled polystyrene tray in the supermarket with something that was once running around in the fields or up the yard. But I feel that many of us owe it to ourselves and farmers all over the world, both livestock and arable, to learn about the processes that create our diets. How can we make conscious decisions about fuelling our bodies if we've no idea what's in our food, or how it reached the shops in the first place?

Something that's helped me in my crusade to understand what I'm shovelling into my gob is comparing eating to haircare (which I also know a bit about). I wouldn't use a bottle of shampoo from a cheap 99p-type store. I'd dread to think about the harsh chemicals, the fillers and how it'd strip my hair and scalp of its natural oils. And yet many of us are fine with eating highly processed sausages because they're sitting under a big red banner that states 'half price'. Most of us don't even glance at the back of the packet to see what's really in them because it reads like a list of gobbledegook anyway. I'm saddened by how many people are forced to shop on price nowadays, not on considerations of quality.

As a nation, we've become disconnected from the food that nourishes us. Children can't join the dots between a chicken nugget and a feathered bird pecking around the yard. (Sixty years ago, they'd have been involved in plucking freshly shot pheasants for their tea.) But schools are hesitant to include 'where your food comes from' in their lesson plans because parents might complain that it's too upsetting for little Tamsin and Archie.

I found this out when a class of eight-year-olds came to visit the farm and asked me if the goats ate McDonald's. I thought, *Oh, my God!* and offered free talks at the local primary school to try to spread some knowledge. They turned me down.

I'm still in the process of making changes to my own dietary habits. As I do, I want to speak about it more to make a difference to others. So, I'm hoping you'll be brave, put on your big-girl pants and go on reading. What follows is a bit of myth-busting. I dedicate this chapter to anyone who wants to begin a journey of discovery, starting with the nitty-gritty, taboo, uncomfortable, misunderstood subject of slaughter.

* * *

'Oh, my God! Are they off to the slaughterhouse?'

The shrill voice over the fence startled both of us. It was a local dog-walker, asking if the two-week-old lambs in our field were about to be killed to go on somebody's plate for Sunday lunch. Chris and I looked at each other in disbelief. But could we truly blame her for not understanding that lambs weigh close to 40 kilos when they go to the abattoir (which is more than a German Shepherd dog)? And that to the untrained eye, they look like adult sheep, not like lambs? No, we could not. This information isn't readily available, and the word 'lamb' is rather misleading. Terms like 'pork', 'beef' and 'mutton' don't help either. It all adds to the web of linguistic confusion over where food comes from.

And it isn't just meat that's the problem: it's everything else connected to the food industry. Farmers' markets are popular and fashionable and attract many customers who like the idea of eating seasonal produce. Except that some of these shoppers then ask the farmers when they'll have avocados for sale. But avocados don't grow in Britain at any time of year – they're all imported. Your avo toast may be healthy, but its carbon footprint is likely to be huge.

The word 'abattoir' comes from the French verb *abat-tre,* meaning *to fell.* It sounds less intimidating and aggressive than 'slaughterhouse'. And my idea of what happens there has changed completely as I've learned about the life cycle of farm animals. Hairdresser Zoë's picture of slaughter was as follows: cold and forbidding concrete buildings that stink of wheelie-bin day in summer. Floors that run with blood. Animals in tiny prison-like cells screaming and jostling around until, finally, a terrifying figure dressed like the beheader in *Robin Hood* comes round and shoots them, and their blood splashes all the other animals and him. All that wasn't just my overactive imagination. I'd seen, as many of us have, a concoction of activist videos on social media, stitched together with snippets from books and films like *Chicken Run* and *Babe*.

I hadn't considered real-life practicalities. An abattoir is a business. It has to run efficiently, and the end product, which means the meat, needs to move smoothly through the process. Surely that can't be the case if an animal ends up dead on the floor in a bloodbath with its brains splattered all around and a load of other panicking animals stamping on it. So – can that really be what happens? My ignorance about this was not unusual. Lots of people just glaze over rather than think it through. The subject of slaughter is also a minefield: who and what do you believe?

As a livestock farmer who uses the internet, I sometimes get online abuse. What I've learned is that people often don't read a single word I've written. They see a photo and go completely bat-shit crazy, sending me messages on social media littered with words like 'murderer' and 'killer'. Now I've certainly done wrong in my life, like the time I accepted an All Saints studded belt from a boyfriend even though I knew he'd nicked it from House of Fraser, or the day I drove the truck uninsured. There are also a few other things I can't go into here as Grandpa Tim will most likely read this book – but think of bored seventeen-year-olds in a dead-end town. Murder, however, I cannot admit to.

These kinds of social-media messages are always aggressive. Most times the poster drops the C-bomb and every word stinks of miseducation. I used to respond, which unfortunately only gave them airtime – they thrive when you bite back. I'd get the prickly rage that comes over you when someone's pushing their trolley at a snail's pace in Morrisons, and I'd just have to reply. My go-to line was always 'Does your cat [there would often be a profile picture of a cat] eat meat?' This mostly got a reply, but the unpleasant exchanges that followed rarely gave me any more satisfaction than hitting my head against a brick wall would have done. So I gave up on the catty exchanges. I refuse to be abused or villainized.

Except . . . I wondered if these people might have a valid point. After all, I'd never set foot inside an abattoir. I'd never witnessed slaughter. How did I know for certain what it was like? Yet the animals I was giving my soul to rear healthily and happily were going to end their lives there. They could have sad eyes and be screaming for all I knew. So I asked Chris whether he'd mind if I went along to watch. I think he was worried that it would freak out my former vegetarian self and send me sprinting back to the salon with my tail between my legs. He agreed, though. He knew better than to try to stop me.

I won't pretend I was casual, calm and collected on the day I first went to the abattoir, because I was the opposite. I knew the lambs weren't going to be shot, because I'd asked Chris about this early on in our relationship. He told me they would be stunned, but that doesn't help when you're clueless. Stunned when? Stunned how? It turned out I was correct that the place was made of concrete – but that was almost all I was correct about. Oh, and during summer, it does smell like wheelie-bin day. What did I expect?

* * *

Trespassers will be prosecuted. CCTV in operation.

These not-very-inviting signs were displayed every few yards as we drove down the track. 'Are you sure we took the right turning, babe?' I asked, and Chris gave me the look he saves for when I ask ridiculous questions during a film.

'This is it. The signs are cos of the activists, Zo. I was

stuck here for two hours last summer with a protest going on. '

We carried on driving. I could hear the clanging of the metal livestock trailer behind us. As one of the ewes on board made a sound, my stomach flipped. I felt dread about what the next hour (*or maybe more? Exactly how long would this take?*) would hold.

All our livestock travel regularly on the trailer throughout their lives. We catch them in pens for worming and fly-spraying and other husbandry before moving them onto fresh grass or over the river for their 'turnip holiday'. This wasn't unusual for them, and they weren't stressed out by it, or no more so than usual. Vets have to sign off that they're fit for slaughter and safe to enter the food chain, so the farm's paperwork is checked on arrival – a movement form stating what animals are on board. (If the trailer is carrying cattle, the vet also checks their ear tag numbers and passports.) An animal can't enter the food chain if it's 'plain', which means too skinny, or if there's a health issue that makes it unfit for human consumption, like a worm infestation, for example. Touch wood, we've never had any of ours condemned.

When the trailer full of ewes and lambs arrived at the abattoir, they were run into a holding pen just like the others they'd been used to. Only about ten at a time went in – far less tightly packed than at the market or when we handle them. Again, it wasn't as stressful as I'd thought it would be. It went like clockwork, in fact. They were perfectly relaxed and it rubbed off on me: I felt my tense, hunched shoulders lower a little. Then the slaughterman came in: rosy cheeks, a long white coat (surprisingly clean, I noted: I wondered which wash he put it on) and white wellies. He carried what can only be described as a giant pair of barbecue tongs with what looked like cotton wool balls on the ends. My mind was racing and I watched him like a hawk, just waiting to see something that would send me off into a spiral of Quorn nuggets and reassessing all of my choices in life.

He was incredibly meticulous as he put the tongs on either side of the first ewe's head – and then she dropped to the floor. No blood, no electrical sparks and really quick. Quicker than I'd ever imagined. I was honestly expecting a degree of suffering. But even after watching the first, I still held my breath in anticipation. *Surely the other sheep will see what's going on? Won't they freak out and start that panicked bleating, like when their lambs stray a bit too far?* This close to death, I was expecting pandemonium. But they didn't bat an eyelid. They didn't seem affected at all. Perhaps they thought that ewe was just taking a nap, lazy mare. She wasn't fitting or twitching on the ground either, in the way animals can do after they've died of natural causes. She was very much gone. Before I knew it, her leg was attached to a pulley system and she was hoisted onto a zip wire that led next door where a different man used a knife to cut her neck so that the blood could drain out of her.

I won't pretend their seamless system didn't feel a bit like the *Saw* movies, and I also don't claim that I wouldn't absolutely shit my knickers if I'd been left alone in there, or if a rogue hair had tickled the back of my neck at any point. This is death, after all: it's never going to feel pleasant. But the ewe knew absolutely nothing about any of it. Then the production line continued with the skinning and gutting of the carcass until the memory of the animal in the field became a little blurred. It's remarkable how quickly this happens. There's a huge amount of craftsmanship and skill involved in the time between the field and the plate. In the modern world, it's something almost nobody sees – I never would have imagined it. A few decades ago, it would have been well-known.

Now, was that better or worse than you expected? It was certainly better for me. A giant weight had been lifted. I hadn't cried or felt queasy or compelled to chain myself to the abattoir gates to stop the lorries driving in, like that time Chris had been held up for two hours. I was at peace with how our animals were killed there, which is why we've used that abattoir ever since, even though it takes at least forty-five minutes to drive there. I wish the distance was shorter.

We have a duty of care to the livestock on our farm. But a hell of a lot of things that happen are out of our control: the weather, market prices, the spread of diseases. What we do control is their death. Of course, nothing dying is ever a nice feeling, whether that's due to natural causes or because the animal was suffering or due to enter the food chain. But the slaughter is certainly humane, and suffering is reduced to a minimum. I'm proud to be part of an industry in the UK that operates to the highest global standards of animal welfare.

* * *

The accident happened in September 2021 on the M25 motorway very close to the Dartford Crossing bridge and tunnel over (and under) the river Thames to the east of London. If you've driven round that section, you'll know how busy it can get and in particular just how many lorries travel that route. The road running north goes through the tunnel, and the high, arched bridge takes the flow of traffic going south.

Chris was in the inside lane, towing a trailer full of sheep, when a lorry in the middle lane clipped the back of the car in front and sent the car sheering straight into his path. He heard a bang and as he looked to his right, for two clear seconds he saw the terrified driver alongside him, fighting for control of his vehicle. The thought passed through Chris's mind that *this could be the last thing I ever see.* Instinctively, he swerved. As he tried to bring the truck and trailer to a controlled stop, there was a second thump as someone rammed into the back of it.

Once he'd managed to come to a halt on the hard

shoulder, his first thought was for the drivers of the other vehicles. He got out of the truck and could see that the guy who'd been driving the car was extremely shaken, just standing there on the tarmac sobbing, but thankfully uninjured.

Immediately, his next thought was for the sheep. How much had the trailer lurched around as the car struck it? His biggest worry was broken legs if his passengers had been thrown about, so he jumped out and did a quick inspection. Everyone was still on four feet and seemed okay. He was also concerned about the accident causing them stress, because flooding their bodies with adrenalin can damage the quality of their meat if they're slaughtered before their bodies have produced enough lactic acid to deal with it: this is partly why everyone involved in transportation and slaughter wants the animals to be calm and relaxed. But they seemed all right, and it's impossible to ask a sheep if it understands that it's been involved in a road accident.

Chris didn't have much time to think about what had happened: he had to get the sheep to the abattoir as their travelling times are strictly controlled by law. Again, this is about making sure that they don't get stressed out by a long journey. He phoned a friend who was kind enough to bring his truck along to tow the trailer onwards within the transit time allowed and the sheep completed their journey with him. (Chris also showed real presence of mind and remembered to ask for a photo of the lorry driver's green card. It made claiming on insurance much easier.)

Our really big problem was the truck, which was written off in the collision. It didn't look like much, with all its dents and scrapes caused by cows and bumps into fence posts, but we loved it. It was more than just a reliable old workhorse: it was our travelling wardrobe, medicine cabinet and storage depot all in one, packed full of ear-taggers, syringes and tools for mending fences, and we'd been counting on another ten years together. But nobody responsible for valuing it was going to agree about that, so there was no chance of us being paid its true value.

Suddenly Chris had minutes to empty it of all our worldly possessions, trying not to leave anything behind, while his whole body jumped and jangled with adrenalin so that it was hard to think clearly. He forgot two pairs of wellies in the end – both mine – and my favourite hat. He eventually arrived home with everything in a cardboard box clutched in front of him, looking like an evacuee.

After all the dramas we had faced rearing those lambs, and all the financial investment they represented, this was the very last step – and something completely out of our control could still go wrong. All we could do was feel thankful that it hadn't been much worse.

* * *

A lot has happened in these last few pandemic years, aside from an increase in the number of keyboard warriors out there. But amid all the death, anxiety and separation we've all been through, there have been a few positives. For example, more consumers have begun to shop locally and to support small businesses.

This growth in the market for locally sourced food gave us the idea to start a direct sales business called The Little Farm Fridge. It's an outlet that allows us to sell our meat directly off the farm to the consumer, which gives us some control over price. That's something you can never get from selling livestock. Prices at the local market fluctuate constantly, and there are big price differences across the country.

It was time to add 'butcher' to our CVs – and hope we could pull it off. Chris had a vague idea of how to dismember a lamb, but I had never seen a carcass being broken down before. Now, with my newly acquired skills, I look back at a New Year's Eve do a few years ago when we spit-roasted a whole 20-kilo lamb to enjoy with our friends, and I'm so embarrassed at the way we just sliced it up to serve. Our craftsmanship with a blade has improved greatly since then: late-night YouTube videos and endless pages of notes on animal anatomy have helped us build enough confidence to have a proper go at butchery. Not bad for a former plumber and a hairdresser who had no kind of training or qualifications in it and have worked very hard to acquire these skills.

The next step in setting up our business was to think about what we would sell. Perfecting our sausage recipes was a painstaking process. At the start it was fun, singing 'Unchained Melody' while piping the meat into the skin (ooh-er, Matron!). Did you know that real sausage skins are made from pigs' intestines? Me neither – until the first time I opened a brined pack and put two and two together as to why they were called 'hog casings'.

But weeks of coming home from a full day's farm-ing then spending four hours getting stuck into sausage-making, often in silence, eyes burning with fatigue, began to take their toll. We spent hours linking sausages only to find out that the mix was too crumbly, or we tasted and discovered (too late!) that our Cumberlands had way too much pepper. We spent two months getting the blasted white-pepper level right and our conclusion was that it's all just too subjective. We'll never agree how much there should be. There were no karaoke versions of the Right-eous Brothers any more, and a couple of times during the after-hours sausage parties (a term I'm using very loosely) we'd catch each other's gaze across the kitchen, full of regret for all those delirious nights in the lambing shed, egging each other on. *Whose absurd idea was this anyway? And what idiot went along with it?* To be honest, I still hate sausage day – which comes round every two weeks – but at least we got it right in the end and they're delicious bangers now.

I've noticed how people are always grabbing on to the 'ex-vegetarian turned farmer and butcher' angle to my story, and on paper I guess it is a full 180. But I was never a vegetarian for animal rights. I chose to eat a vegetarian diet because I couldn't afford anything that even vaguely resembled quality meat and because I was still struggling with my vomiting phobia. The way I look at it, the biggest difference between vegetarian-hairdresser-Zoë and Zoë-with-the-butcher's-knife is that now I understand exactly where my food comes from. I make decisions based on that.

Getting The Little Farm Fridge going was tough. Both of us felt rather out of our depth in the business aspects, but determined to get to grips with it. After all, look how far we'd come. We were also in the Covid pandemic (hence the surge of interest in supporting local businesses like ours), but although the timing was still challenging in many ways, we felt we needed to strike while the iron was hot.

In the pandemic chaos, all the local council offices had closed and their staff were working from home. That meant we sat for hours on hold on the phone as we tried to get through to whoever could advise us. Building supplies were like gold dust because people who were off work on furlough seized the chance to do DIY and home improvements. But then, among all the upheaval and uncertainty, came a gift sent from above: our bank offered us a loan to help our business bounce back. The amount made our eyes water, but the money would also allow us to plan and progress with more certainty.

Getting the business going was *full on* – and we were tending a fully stocked farm as well. One day we'd be laying the concrete pad for the chiller (without a mixer, may I add), the next we were shearing the ewes. The day after that we were making our spiced goat burgers in the morning to trial the new burger presses, and in the afternoon worming the cattle. We had to dig deep to pull it out of the bag. I think someone must have pumped us full of speed – it was the only way we could keep going. But, hey, we can sleep when we're dead.

At the time, the only part I felt I truly excelled at was the branding and customer relations – that is, choosing what colour paper bags we should use to pack up our goods, and chatting. (*You can take the girl out of Soho, but you can't take Soho out of the girl*, I thought.) But, looking back, I see that I'm being too hard on myself. I also built our fully functioning website with no previous experience and a strong dislike for computers, following the excellent instructions on a build-your-own-platform site. Every time a sale pings through on it, my first instinct is that the website must have malfunctioned and I've just charged an innocent customer four grand instead of forty quid due to a faulty payment form I created at 11 p.m. after a heavy day. But it hasn't happened yet. All has gone well, and if I'm feeling down, I sometimes have a browse around the site just to give myself a little ego massage. I don't always feel like I'm capable, but this achievement proves I am.

Adding the shop into the mix has also given us a payday each month, which is liberating. Neither of us particularly enjoys the butchering side of the business, but it brings us a little extra security. We're very proud of our product: it's high welfare, grass fed, and the care and time we take in raising our animals really does show in the quality. There's nothing like a customer telling us that ours is the best lamb they've ever tasted.

I won't gloss over the fact that running a new business has been less than smooth sailing at times. There have been screaming rows over packaging, and sleepless nights fretting about whether someone's wedding order that I've sent off with the courier is going to arrive in one piece. But as I write, The Little Farm Fridge is now in her second year of operation. That's a risky period for lots of small businesses: it's when more than a fifth of start-ups fail, so getting past this milestone is an achievement we're proud of.

As we plan ahead with The Little Farm Fridge, we think about our customers. What kind of meat do people like to eat? And what might they want next year, or the year after that?

In the past, the cheapest parts of an animal, called offal – the entrails and internal organs – would usually be eaten by the poorest people. Nowadays they're served up to the wealthiest, and dishes like crispy pig's cheek, grilled ox heart and devilled kidneys appear on the menus of fashionable restaurants. (Super-ironic or what?) But apart from places like that, these products aren't commonly seen on supermarket shelves in the UK. Lack of demand for certain animal parts in Britain means that more of each carcass is wasted, which costs us money as farmers because we have to pay to have it removed.

Other cultures are far thriftier, cooking with the heart, liver and kidneys, and finding innovative ways to use most of the animal, like stuffing and braising the intestines, making broth from bones and even using the paddywhack – the tough tendon that holds the animal's head up, like a thick elastic rope that resembles exercise bands. It doesn't make my stomach rumble but it's very popular in Chinese cuisine, as are chicken feet. When I worked in Soho, I'd often find myself in tucked-away corner shops buying cigarettes and it was like being transported abroad – I saw delicacies I'd never come across in the UK before. There were Indian sweets and pastries, and sometimes unidentifiable objects with zero recognizable words printed on the front. That's the beautiful thing about big cities.

I'm absolutely sure that if I was served offal properly cooked, by those who know what they're doing, it would be delicious. But I still have issues about eating it – my phobia about sickness, again, casting its old shadow of control over me. It's rather childish, and I don't like to be so closed to trying something new, but it's part of my personality. And, of course, I'm not alone. For many different reasons, lots of people in this country are the same. Take using bones in cooking, for example. In The Little Farm Fridge, we try to sell as many bones as possible, but Britain seems to have an aversion to meat on the bone. Most other cultures wouldn't dream of preparing a curry or a stew without the bones to add more flavour.

But the price of meat is rising, and I think all of us will have to be more resourceful with what we serve. Cheaper cuts, like rolled lamb breast and beef skirt, are already becoming more popular, and I believe it won't be too long before offal will make a comeback. It won't happen overnight, and as I'm writing this, I'm feeling like the biggest hypocrite ever because I can't think of anything worse than eating organs – like the liver and the kidneys – that actually cleaned their original owner's blood. I haven't persevered yet to learn how to make them delicious. A greater demand for offal would mean less food waste from our farm – and just imagine the British public eating fewer imported steaks from Brazil and more home produce. That would be great for the planet. We need a popular media chef on the case – someone like Jamie Oliver – to help offal to catch on.

Many of us will also need confidence and skill in the kitchen – the know-how to cook these dishes. No one is to blame if they don't have it – you can't know what you've never been taught – but we need to bring this knowledge back. When a farming friend suggested to me recently that I contact the local food bank to find out if they had food waste that we could feed to the animals, I was really surprised to hear that a food bank might have anything left over. The guy who ran the place explained that they did. The food no one wanted was the fresh stuff, he said. The food bank's users couldn't make it into meals. Lately, I think that there are worries about cooking costs as well: anything that means you have to use the oven for any length of time makes people scared about their fuel bill. Shocking, right? I walked away from the food bank that day with 3 kilos of pheasant breast meat that nobody wanted: they didn't know what to do with it. That's a problem we, as a society, need to solve.

At The Little Farm Fridge, we try to use as much of each animal as we can to limit our wastage: our 'nose to tail' ethos. One example of this is our plan to use the intestines of the same animal that the sausage meat filling came from to make the sausage skin. We'd also like a licence to get the sheepskins and goat hides back from the abattoir, then to have them crafted into rugs. Or we could have our goat skins tanned and made into wallets, even. I just wish there were more hours in a day for us to explore these possibilities – and, of course, it will take money to invest and expand our business.

We don't sell any chicken and we're often asked why. The answer is that it's just not a feasible meat for us to farm. We're infested with foxes: chickens and foxes are not good cohabiters. Not many people know this but there's little to no profit from rearing chickens, plucking and gutting them. It's therefore not a commercial direction we would go in.

We're fortunate to have built up all our social media followers over the years and it's given us a public platform, a voice. I'd like to use that voice to make people think about what they're eating. Chris and I have already begun to do this. Lots of companies – even major supermarkets – use 'influencers' (people who post content on social media and have lots of followers) and we saw that one was posting wild claims about how a supermarket's new plant-based burger was great for the environment. To state this for certain, you need lots of information: what's in a product, where it was produced, how far it's been transported and many other precise details. Many people can't or don't engage with all this in a fact-checking kind of way. But the influencer was in a paid partnership with the supermarket and she should have done her homework before she accepted and supported its message. Chris challenged her 'environmentally friendly' claim and the Advertising Standards Authority, which lays down the rules advertisers have to follow and can take action against misleading ads, got involved. Eventually the influencer took down her post.

I want to stand strong on what we as farmers do in the UK, not pussyfoot around subjects that might be uncomfortable such as what happens in a slaughterhouse. I would also like to challenge the disregard shown by parts of the population when it comes to the meat in our fridges. It should be butchered and cooked with care, and we should savour the taste and the nutritional energy it's providing. Animals should be treated with respect to the very end, when the time comes for them to take on their role in the food chain, to nourish humans.

When Covid 19 turned the world upside down, life felt precarious and uncertain. Yet farmers all over the country continued working tirelessly, as we always do, to keep the nation fed. I can only hope that the pandemic might have brought a new appreciation of our work.

I was so disconnected from the origins of food when I first started farming. I'm not ashamed to admit how removed I was from what I was putting into my body. Brussels sprouts come from Australia, avocados from South America, tomatoes from Saudi Arabia. All perfectly normal, right? I didn't even check the egg box to see where the eggs came from – just the cheapest price tag would do.

This isn't a dig at you if the origin of your food isn't high on your list of priorities. We all have different agendas and sometimes people's finances don't stretch far enough. Now, with the cost-of-living crisis in the headlines, it's getting even harder. People need to survive and put food in their children's bellies. But if you *are* able to think about it, there are small changes you can make and these will start to add up as more and more of us make them. We can find out which foods are seasonal and choose those items more often. None of us knows this automatically: even years into finding out about food production, I'm still learning. After a while, it can become second nature. It's the same with air miles: look at the country of origin, then give the products from the other side of the Earth a miss and spread the information.

I've been fortunate enough to pick up my knowledge during the past few years, and now I want to share it. After all, our planet is in crisis. Devastating bushfires, tsunamis and earthquakes are Mother Nature's warning to humans that we're close to the edge of keeping Earth liveable. But small steps taken by lots of people could become the norm. Wouldn't it be nice to feel that we're trying to help, even having an impact, however tiny?

There's no need to break the bank by doing this, either. Just be more conscious. One idea is to eat high welfare meat but cheaper cuts: instead of rump steak that was reared in what used to be part of the Amazon rainforest, try a rolled brisket from your local farm. Or eat meat fewer times in a week. We can't create new lifestyles or new eating habits overnight but we can try to do a little better.

Cutting down food waste is a huge passion for Chris and I: we want to take small steps and encourage others if and where we can. I'm not a saint – and I'm still partial to an avocado – but this is what I believe so I carry on the campaign. I'd love you to join me.

* * *

As I hurried across the hayfield, I could see the lamb struggling on the ground. She'd tried to get into the pear orchard, as so many of them do – they love pears. (I'd estimate that 20 per cent of our time is spent fetching sheep back from places they shouldn't be – in our neighbour's garden, down the road in the village, in the garden of a pub a mile away.) But she'd caught her leg in the netting, and as she thrashed about, she had pulled part of the fence over and failed to extricate herself. She was one of the wild breeds too, and as I crouched beside her to free her, I knew she'd probably fight me. I pulled her clear of the netting as gently as I could. As she scrambled to her feet, I was hoping she'd run off and be okay, but the worst harm wasn't to the fence. She'd done some damage to herself, and couldn't put her weight on one of her back legs.

Sheep that fall over sometimes get stuck on their backs or their sides and can hurt themselves badly trying to get right. I've seen horns knocked off, which leads to loads of bleeding, and then it's very difficult to keep flies away. Sheep that can't get up can also seriously injure their heads from banging them on the ground. As I looked more closely at this girl, I could see she was in trouble: she must have been struggling a lot, and the angle of that leg as it dangled underneath her just made my stomach churn. It was obviously broken but not cleanly: the break was a splintery mess.

She wasn't making any sound, but that's not unusual:

sheep in distress are more likely to grind their teeth. As I watched her stagger off, I could see she was suffering. Still, it might just heal, I thought, and a three-legged sheep can survive. Maybe the vet could come and put on a cast. But when an injury looks as mangled as that one, I knew that the mending process would be difficult. It would be impossible to get her to keep still, and with every movement she made, the damage would get worse.

It's cruel to leave her to suffer when the situation's not likely to improve, or to put her through treatment that wouldn't have a good outcome. I hate to think of our animals in pain. (Somehow for me the idea of them being left thirsty is the worst thing of all: thirst is such a torment – much worse than hunger.) I phoned Chris and explained. A decision like that would need a double vote.

'It's a bit of a car-crash accident, babe. She's not looking good at all.'

As soon as Chris saw her, he agreed. We needed to dispatch her as quickly as we could. A sick or poisoned lamb can't go into the food chain, of course, but this one was perfectly healthy. If we wanted to send her to the abattoir, though, we'd need to get our vet to come, to witness how she died and complete all the paperwork. After that, we'd have to arrange transportation – and, of course, we'd be paying for all that. Any visit by a vet to the farm, even just to give an injection, will cost us at least two hundred pounds. Our other option was to dispatch her ourselves, then prepare and butcher her on the farm for our own table. It was the only decision we could make.

'Thank you, sweetheart,' Chris said to the lamb. If a creature has suffered and he's acting to bring their suffering to an end, he'll also say, 'Sorry, sweetheart.' Saying thank you to an animal for its life is something we always do on the farm. Without them, we'd have nothing. Our sheep give us lambs to earn us a living. They look after us. The least we can do is to make sure we never take them for granted.

Once the lamb was gone, we worked together to prepare the carcass to eat. When I first became a shepherd, I couldn't eat lamb during lambing. The smell of amniotic fluid is a lot like the smell of their meat, and by the end of each day, my hands would smell like lamb. Then Chris said something that helped me see this in a more holistic way: 'It's a cycle, Zo. All our energy goes into looking after them and protecting them, and then they give that energy to us. Nothing gets wasted. We should be thankful for that.' I've accepted and understood this now. Knowing exactly how our animals have lived and how they died has completely changed my relationship with food.

As we prepared the carcass, I thought, *This is like being outside time. It's what all the generations that came before us did, and how they survived. They lived far closer to the land, connected to the cycles of birth and death in a way that we have lost.* Not many people eat like this, and we were honoured to be able to do so. We don't whittle our animals' bones into cutlery or use their ballsacks as purses (our forebears would certainly have done both), but as we worked, we felt the same reverence for life that they must have felt. There's something inherently primal about this practice. It's not something I ever imagined myself taking part in, or even witnessing, but as I did so, I felt somehow privileged to be a part of the ritual. 'Ritual' really is the word. The whole event felt almost sacred. We were eerily quiet and did everything slowly (although maybe that was because we were still learning how to carry out the job) and as I worked, I felt a sense of connection to my ancestors – to those who paved the way throughout time.

I found a deeper meaning too: this lamb had been born and reared on this farm and the cycle of its living and dying was completed in one place. That was once normal, but in the modern world, it's rare. It showed me the circle of life and helped me truly understand that I'm a part of it. This is how I think now about the losses, gains and continuous nature of survival, especially through the life of a farmer. In the end, we are all a part of something greater.

Bubble with Sheep

'How mental is it in Italy with the pandemic?'

'It's insane. They've just lost control. Hospitals running out of space. All those patients they can't treat.'

It was Chris's birthday and we had his whole family round for a Chinese to celebrate. But in February 2020 there could be only one topic of conversation. With Italy in full pandemic crisis and the new Covid-19 virus advancing everywhere, just how worried should we be? For someone who struggles with health anxiety anyway, a silent attack from a virus had all my worst fears playing out. And now my health issues weren't only in my head: they were feeding off this whole global emergency.

'The virus is bound to come to this country. It's probably here already,' Chris's stepdad pointed out.

'In Italy you have to get a permit to leave your house,'
said his mum.

Chris and I looked at each other.

'Do you actually think that could happen here?' I asked
her.

There was silence. Then she answered, 'I don't know.
But it's looking pretty hairy.'

Chris was shaking his head. 'Me and Zoë couldn't stay
inside,' he said. 'Not with the farm. It's not possible.'

'But what if one of you catches the coronavirus?' his
mum said. 'Or both of you together? You couldn't work
then. Maybe you need to make a plan.'

Even in normal times, life is tricky if Chris or I get
sick. He still suffers autoimmune flare-ups from time to
time, and although he doesn't give in to them easily, he
listens to his body, taking a day or so's rest if he needs
to. But if Chris was out of action for longer than that,
I couldn't manage on my own, and while he's obviously
the more experienced farmer of the two of us, I also
think he'd struggle without me. 'Farmer' is such a simple
word, but it's a super-high-adrenalin job and the skills
it requires are sometimes close to superhuman: driving
round the fields with eyes everywhere, fifteen minutes
to check everyone's on four feet and doing okay, then to
get the trailer loaded and on the road because an unforeseen circumstance has made you late. Life is pretty much

a series of unforeseen circumstances making you late, which can always be traced back to an animal doing something inconvenient.

Before we'd even had breakfast the other morning, we'd been first-aiders, groomers, mothers, playdates, builders, plumbers, chefs and comforters for our animals, and that's why taking any time away from the farm requires serious planning. Finding someone to take your place is incredibly hard. You never quite trust anyone else with your livestock as much as you trust yourself. It's like your eyebrow lady or a decent barber: after five decent threading appointments in a row, you finally feel safe in their hands.

That's why Chris and I have spent more than one night away together just twice in five years. (My avoidance of holiday risk-of-infection horrors, which still bothers me from time to time, means that I'm not too fussed about that.) But our very first joint holiday, when we finally went camping with some friends for five whole days, was when I realized just how difficult it was going to be *ever* to leave the farm. I opened my eyes on our first morning. It was quiet, and the sun was already shining outside the tent. I could just roll over and sleep some more if I felt like it – there was nothing very urgent to get up for. Except I suddenly found I couldn't.

Because today I wouldn't be checking every corner of every field, every hotspot where the sheep like to get their heads stuck. I wouldn't be feeding the Pygmy goats their breakfast first (otherwise they bully everyone else off theirs). I wouldn't be making sure that Effie had her pallet covered with straw because she doesn't like sleeping on the floor. Not having all this work to do might sound relaxing – but instead I felt an enormous wave of guilt about leaving the farm at all, followed by an even bigger wave of sheer dread at all the things that might go wrong in our absence. I assume this is something like leaving a child with its grandparents while you steal a night at a spa hotel that you got as a Christmas present eighteen months ago.

The vulnerability of our business preys on our minds. It's why I made the decision to put my health and good nutrition front and centre once I became a full-time farmer. When you're working hard and asking a lot of your body, it needs some TLC. Not to provide it is a fast track to savage burnout. Chris is just as careful as I am: managing his illness has made him an absolute pro at watching for signs of trouble. At the start of our relationship, he was so unwell that he was bed-bound. Now he never takes for granted his freedom to leave the house. He makes every hour – every minute – of daylight count; both of us squeeze the productivity out of it. We've had some comments and judgements about this down the years: 'You two work too hard,' and 'You'll burn yourselves out if you're not careful.' Still, we always choose to seize the day.

But when the Covid-19 virus came, it was the Joker: a

completely unpredictable malign new force that no one could contain, spreading and mutating at a ghastly rate. If Chris went down with it – and his autoimmune condition made him super-vulnerable – or if we both got it, we had no staff to fall back on. Our farming friends have their own farms, which take up all their time, so there'd be nobody to take care of our livestock and livelihood. Our animals would be left without water, the young ones without food and in messy bedding, the goats caught up in the fence with no one to extricate them. It wasn't worth thinking about. And lambing was just around the corner – our most financially critical time. How well the lambing season goes dictates how much money we'll have for the rest of the year. Everything hinges on it.

'We can't catch the coronavirus, Zo,' Chris said, later on that night.

'Nope. We can't. We need to make a plan.'

'Shall we try to get a caravan at the farm?' he suggested. 'So we can isolate – just the two of us?'

From the moment he said it, I was fully on board. There was no official lockdown announcement yet, but things were looking bad. The only way to be sure that we could protect our health and our business was to go right off-grid. For how long? We didn't know. We had no idea what was coming – but back in March 2020, neither did anybody else.

* * *

'What about this one?' I asked.

Chris leaned over my shoulder and we peered at the screen. 'Where is it exactly?'

'Not too far. We could get down there in less than an hour.'

'Looks good. Shall we ring them?'

'Yep.' I grabbed the phone.

We were frantically scrolling eBay for caravans and this one was within our budget – tight as ever – and just a forty-minute drive away. We hadn't read the ad all that carefully, but what the hell?

The second we saw the caravan, the decision was made. Her name was 'Compass Corona' – and if that's not a sign, will somebody please tell me what is? I didn't even bother looking inside and Chris might have opened a cupboard or two half-heartedly. Then we handed over two grand and hooked her up to the truck.

'Did we check the toilet was working?' I asked, as we drove back in thoughtful silence.

'Um, not really,' Chris said.

'Any idea how we get the shower to come on? Or connect up the power?'

'Nah.'

'Have we actually lost our minds, do you think?'

But this felt like our first house together. New home-owners are always euphoric, and nothing could touch us. We towed her home and set up camp. A quick scrub round, and we were ready to move in, with the smell of Zoflora gracing our nostrils. What a time to be alive.

* * *

On 23 March 2020, as the first national lockdown began, we retreated from the chaos into Compass Corona. To start with, our plan had been to put our new caravan out in one of the fields. The thought of living in the open like that was appealing at first, but the more we thought about it, the more problems we could see. We'd be open to the weather, kept awake by wind and rain, and we'd have to build a shelter to keep our boots in because we certainly couldn't store them outdoors. So we asked our landlady, who rents us the hay barn, if we could park it in there. She was fine with it and for the next two months we never left except to get fuel for our vehicles (strictly paying at the pump).

Compass Corona was a very basic place, providing what we needed and no more: we could cook, eat, wash and sleep. The whole experience of living there felt primal. We ate our own meat, along with vegetables and fruit from the farm shop our landlady owns. The extra chores that caravan life required should have made our life more difficult, but we quickly got used to the routines of filling up the clean-water drum and emptying the waste water. As we accepted and embraced them, we found they could even be a joy. The lack of a flushing toilet also led to a conversation I'd never imagined with a partner: the waste-water tank had to be emptied every other day and the person who did this would see the other's poos. This was a whole new level of intimacy. In the end, I opted for that chore. It showed me what a long way I'd come from the days when I'd listen to J.Lo and dream up my chocolate-box life plan for romance.

The caravan is frankly a bit of a dive. It's so cramped that when you're sitting on the loo, your feet are in the shower tray so your socks get soaking wet if you get up for a pee in the night. The stove is right next to the bed – you can reach over and open the oven door while you're still lying down. For the first few weeks I was really puzzled about why I was suddenly getting acne, but then I realized that Chris's bacon cooking in the morning was spitting grease all over my pillow. The sink pulls down – a bit like the tray on an aeroplane except it has a dip in it for water – and when you've washed you flip it up and the waste water drains down the back. But if you've left anything on the sink – like your soap – it goes tumbling into the abyss. We must have lost a nail brush down there every week.

But it was somewhere I also felt immensely protected. We were lambing and we'd always be up early – very early – in the darkness before dawn. Lots of lambs are born at sunrise, and when the rush was over, by mid-morning, we'd come back to Compass Corona and have a mug of hot chocolate in the peace of the hay barn. When I'm really old, I'll look back at that memory and see us sitting there together, hands warmly wrapped around the comfort of those drinks. The world was going up in flames and there we were in our safe place, protected in a bubble with sheep.

* * *

Every single night at ten o'clock, though, the scary outside world would break in. Chris wanted to watch the news because he felt that we had to keep on top of what was happening outside and the progress of the pandemic. But it was so hypnotically bad that I almost didn't want to know. Each evening as we turned on, things grew worse. The rate of Covid infections kept rising and rising. So many people were suffering.

Before the pandemic started, we'd learned to love the isolation of our farming life. It was something we were used to, and we also had each other. But now we knew that many were completely alone, and not by choice. We had wide spaces all around us – a hundred acres to walk in – while friends who lived in cities in small flats were allowed outside just once a day for a walk close to their home. Of course we missed our families, but we had their support and we never worried about running out of anything because my mum dropped supplies, like toothpaste, in our driveway. We weren't making any money – which was extremely stressful – but we were able to manage. Many had lost their livelihoods entirely.

Quite often I would find myself thinking about the old boys at the market. Market day is when they meet their friends, and for some it's probably their main time for social interaction. Everything had stopped, so who did they have to meet or speak to? We heard through the grapevine about senior farmers being terribly affected, and well-known members of the community felt lost: a lovely guy called Roy whom we see regularly at the market got Covid really badly and his illness dragged on for months. He still isn't back to the way he was. One problem in agriculture is that people often keep working well past the usual retirement age, which leaves them very vulnerable. The virus cut a swathe through so many people's lives, disrupting familiar patterns that just weren't easy for the older generations to pick up again afterwards.

It was the weirdest and scariest time, but I knew I was lucky. For so many, the pandemic was a nightmare of loneliness and fear, and for some it had the bleakest of endings.

* * *

'What on earth's she doing?' Chris muttered.

'Don't ask me, babe,' I whispered back.

The woman was sitting cross-legged in the middle of the field on a picnic blanket with her eyes tightly closed.

The backs of her hands were resting on her kneecaps with palms facing up and fingers delicately extended. She was wearing headphones and a serene expression.

'I think she's meditating,' I told him.

'Aaah. Right. She looks pretty chill,' Chris said.

I took a harder line. 'She looks like she's trespassing!'

'So what do we do? Do we interrupt her? Shall we make a noise?'

We were weeks into lockdown and getting used to people leaving the public footpaths that give them right of way across our land. We knew how lucky we were not to be confined indoors, and sympathized with anyone who didn't have much space at home or who was simply feeling stir crazy. But our fields – apart from the footpath – were private property, and exploring land where livestock are grazing isn't always safe.

Unfortunately, some of our visitors had also started treating the farm like a park. It was especially difficult not to be angry with those who dumped litter or let their dogs off the leash. Eventually, some areas had such heavy footfall that it wasn't safe to put sheep there – but by now it was the busiest part of the lambing season and we were coping with forty births a day, trying to move the ewes around to keep particular areas clean. Eventually, we found one way to deal with our trespassing problem: we hand-fed our hippie Highland cattle with the long curved horns, with bits of bread which we knew they really liked. This encouraged them to head towards anyone who arrived in the field on foot, hoping for more snacks. The Highlands are gentle free spirits but they can look quite intimidating, and they definitely freaked out a few walkers. It was the best deterrent we could come up with.

* * *

To start with, there were only two rules in the Compass Corona: no farm animals inside, and no dog on the bed. On day two, we broke the dog rule. And I think it was day four or day five when Chris plonked hypothermic lamb triplets on the doormat at 4.30 a.m. This was how caravan life would go. They'd been born on a wild, wet night during a hard frost. Triplets are usually smaller and weaker anyway, and that's a real recipe for disaster. I've never jumped out of bed so fast, springing into nurse mode.

All three were very frail. The weakest lamb was out cold, and as I laid my fingers on its tiny chest, I could feel that its heartbeat was extremely faint. The other two could (just about) hold their heads up. If a lamb can't do that, there is no point in putting a tube into its belly to try to feed it with colostrum.

Only one thing could work here – a lamb oven. It's basically a very large bucket with a hole in it and straw at the bottom. You point a fan heater into it, and then you pop a lid on. Over the years, we've had to get creative when we're devising these ovens – it's nice to use a proper heat lamp but the bulbs get smashed so easily that they haven't lasted more than a few days into the lambing season. Now we use what's available.

We tried our best, but two hours later we had only one survivor. She had floppy dopey ears and the softest, huskiest voice I've heard on a lamb to this day – sometimes they can sound quite shouty. We named her Gyoza and I became her surrogate mother. The ground was dry enough by now for me to drive my trusty Honda CRV 4x4 round the fields to check for lambers and Gyoza would come along with me, curled up on the heated leather seat in the front and taking milk breaks every four hours. I was needed round the clock for her survival, and if I was slow and sleepy with her night feeds, her screams of hunger would wake Chris and Indie. She was a character, all right, and such a comfort in the uncertainty and anxiety of the pandemic when we were being told not to hug our mums and to cancel our weddings.

The pandemic also brought us Olive, the gentlest goat that ever lived. She's a pure-bred Anglo Nubian – the silky ones with spaniel ears that come in a whole range of colours, blacks, browns, smoky greys, almost like camouflage – and she's named after Olive Oyl from *Popeye* for her long spindly legs. Chris loves the Anglo Nubians – we call them Noobs – in the same way that I love the Pygmies: we keep them for pleasure and because they're beautiful, not just as part of the business for their meat and milk. The Noobs and the Pygmies were all in the barn just outside the caravan, so we could be with them when they kidded. We got used to the noises they made: at nights goats definitely snore, and sometimes they argue.

She was one of Noob quadruplets born in the spring of 2021. It's the only time any animal of ours had quads, and Chris was especially delighted when all four turned out to be girls: it meant we could keep them and develop our Noob herd. Their markings were beautiful and they had those gorgeous long Nubian ears, incredibly soft and velvety, almost like baby rabbits. We decided to take two off their mother because goats have just two teats (even though they're usually very milky, this means that only two of the kids would really thrive) and by 2 a.m. on the night that they'd arrived, everyone seemed settled. The two had been fed their colostrum and we all went to bed. An hour or so later I was up again for another feed, and I thought that one of the kids was looking a bit puffy. But perhaps she hadn't had a poo yet: the first poo is called meconium and it's important because it gets everything working properly. I wondered if she needed an enema and decided that there was enough time to wait until morning.

At dawn she wouldn't suck from the bottle. She looked unhappy and very bloated, as though there might be some sort of blockage. As I peered at her, a random thought popped into my mind: *What if she doesn't have a bumhole*? Unfortunately, it's something that can happen. When the four kids were first born, we'd checked very quickly for their sex, basically just feeling in the half-light for bollocks because you don't want to upset the mother of a newborn by overly touching her offspring. Now I checked much more thoroughly, and my heart sank so hard I could have thrown up. There were no holes at all, only a completely smooth surface, like a vulva on a Barbie. We quickly rang the vet. She explained that if an animal is male and the problem is just that there's no bum opening, it's possible to break the skin because everything else is in place. But the chances of doing this for a female are very slim. There's so much going on with female anatomy that an operation would be too complicated and there would be a high risk of infection.

'It's your call,' the vet said, 'but this kid's going to die anyway so I'd think about putting her down to prevent her suffering.'

We sat in total silence. This beautiful young animal was healthy, and she deserved to live. The whole thing was horrific. Having to do this upset us so much that we could hardly bear to think about it; we can hardly talk about it even now. Her sister's death also left Olive by herself (the other two were with their mother), and goats are very stressy and highly strung anyway; change bothers them. She pined for her siblings and obviously hated being alone. It was as though she was under a black cloud – she would hyperventilate with stress and refused to drink her milk. As much as I could, I kept her with me to try to calm her down.

Even when Olive got a bit older and stronger, her chest was still very rattly and she kept needing anti-inflammatories. We gave her our best care: Chris would feed her, I was in charge of medicines; and on we went until she caught a stomach virus when she was five months old. Over the next two days she got weaker, dehydrated and lethargic, until it was obvious she didn't have very long, so I brought her home into the warm so she could die there. There was no crying in pain: she never made a fuss and was just the politest goat you could ever meet. In the end she died quite peacefully. But the following year, when two more tiny Noobs arrived in the pet pen, I noticed that Chris couldn't bear to say how much he liked them. He's still troubled by what happened, afraid that if he feels that way again, he'll spread some kind of jinx and they will die. This is where loving very deeply has its drawbacks.

By the time we'd been nursing Olive, we'd had so much going on in Compass Corona: Roo the Pygmy goat was in a dog crate, Indie was in her bed and Olive was sleeping under ours. The 'no animals in the caravan' rule was going really well, but caring for them all made me certain about my choices in life: after years spent in hairdressing, I had found exactly where I was meant to be.

This feeling has stayed with me. Even though living in the caravan did make extra work and burned up even more energy at our busiest time of year, we thrived on it so much that we decided to live there each spring during lambing. It's partly the convenience: we're right where our animals need us. But it's more than that. Living in such a simple way has brought real peace, even when the pandemic was raging around us and the whole world seemed out of control. One night in Compass Corona, Chris turned to me and said, 'How did we end up here, like this?' I didn't answer – just grinned.

At last I know exactly who I am, I thought.

* * *

After the worst of the pandemic, I, like the rest of the world, was looking forward to the end of cracked hands from sanitizer and antibacterial soap.

'Lambing soon,' Chris said to me. He knew how much I come alive with the buzz and adrenalin of those crazy, intense weeks. Except that in 2021, I didn't. It felt different. Somehow there was no buzz. Something had changed.

The change took place quite gradually at first. At two o'clock one morning, I suddenly sat bolt upright in bed. I was sweating. The anxiety fog swirled in my head and my chest was very tight. I could feel panic taking over. My legs started shaking uncontrollably until I was worrying that it would wake Chris. My teeth began to chatter. I cleared my throat, trying to keep calm. I cleared it again, and then again, until it felt like a tic, but it still wasn't helping me.

I tried to go through a list of things that help. *Pop in a piece of chewing gum and focus on the steady feel of chewing. Breathe in for five, hold for five, then release for six until you feel the pressure in your diaphragm and your stomach goes outwards. Not working? Play an alphabet game – let's try fashion! A for Armani, B for Balenciaga, C for Chanel . . . Nope, I'm still spiralling.*

Don't reach for the diazepam, Zoë, I said to myself. I had some in my drawer, prescribed long ago to help with my anxiety about flying. *You got this.*

Maybe I feel sick because I have food poisoning. What did I have for dinner? Might I actually be sick? Oh, God, not that. And if I start being sick at 2 a.m. I'll never be well enough to work tomorrow. Maybe it's just indigestion. Shit – the only packet of Gaviscon we have is in the truck.

I pulled out my scrunchie and tied it again, making sure my hair was out of the way in case I really did throw up.

C'mon, Zo. You don't need a diazepam.

'Indie darling, please get off my leg – I can't move.' I hung one leg outside the covers so I didn't feel so trapped. But now my sweat had gone cold and I was shivering even more. *Wish I had a thermometer to check I don't have a fever.*

I'd woken Chris. 'Zo?' he said sleepily. 'Zo? What's going on?'

Shit. I give up. I reached into the bedside cabinet for the tablets.

To start with, I hoped this was an isolated event, but then it happened again. And again – until it was almost nightly in the run-up to lambing. The panic attacks could range from mild to a level where I was crouched on the end of the bed convinced I was about to die. And although I kept trying to break the cycle, the panics started earlier and earlier until before too long they set in at 8 p.m. That meant I'd be lucky to sleep through the night, which left me a shell of myself the next day. I didn't want to get out of bed. I wasn't interested in breakfast. I'd snap at Chris and finally drag my feet along to the farm.

I knew that I was sucking the joy out of the atmosphere around me. I'd become a literal mood-hoover. I couldn't remember the last time I'd belly-laughed. I felt an irritability and anger I'd never experienced before, always simmering and threatening to boil over at the most inopportune moments, laced with tears and a prickle of constant nervous energy deep in my belly. Zero pleasure in life, zero fun, no jokes or laughter. I was double-perioding every month and felt as though I'd rather clean the oven than have sex. Let's be honest, every relationship suffers when the sex is dwindling – not saying this is right, but it's chemistry.

The reasons why I thought about Chris leaving me were starting to stack up and I think he was a saint for remaining in the caravan. I knew I was coming across as a vile human being – I knew it deep in my soul but

I couldn't stop it. My black mood was relentless, seeping into everything, every single day. One thought that constantly circled in my head was that, as a child, I'd resented my parents because I hadn't been allowed to have pets and always fantasized about finding abandoned puppies who thought I was their mother. But now I had a pen full of lambs and goats who really *did* think that. I even had a Pygmy goat kid the size of a kitten that I carried in my pocket. My dreams had literally come true – so why wasn't I happy? Why, instead, was I sinking deeper every day into a dark, lonely hole? How do you make sense of that?

The mounting tension all blew up with a huge barney between me and Chris in the shed one morning. The whole road probably heard. It ended with me screaming: '*I don't want to be here any more!*' Chris knew immediately that I didn't mean 'on the farm'. He also understood that what I said didn't have anything to do with him. 'Inside my brain' was the place where I didn't want to be. He suggested I talk to our GP, and I knew he was right.

All the Covid restrictions were still in place and when I got to the surgery, I had to leave my wellies at the door to avoid walking twenty types of bacteria into a sterile environment. Then – dressed in odd socks – I went into the wrong room. My *pièce de résistance* was hopping straight onto the bed rather than sitting in the chair, like a regular human would have done. The GP asked me some questions and when I mentioned having two periods each month, he said he needed to examine me: time for the plastic speculum and lube. Then he told me I had a lump on my cervix and that this would need investigation.

A few minutes later, I was sitting outside in the car and I genuinely thought: *Oh, my God, I'm going batshit because I've got cancer. Perhaps it's affecting all my brain chemicals. Perhaps I'll have to have my uterus removed and Chris will leave me for someone who can give him children.*

I was sent for a colposcopy, but they didn't find any abnormal cells and I was given the all-clear. Not only that, but when the man doing the test found out I was a farmer, it turned out that he wanted some goat meat – so I sold him some right there. Every cloud, eh? But my GP also discussed my anxiety, and the decision that helped me most following this crisis was to start taking antidepressants.

My new friend citalopram has made such a difference. It's a medicine that treats low mood and panic attacks, and three months later I was feeling so much better. The cervical lump turned out to be nothing to worry about and the two-periods-a-month problem was sorted with a quick course of treatment. So I still had a uterus and a boyfriend – and I was free. I don't feel trapped inside my head any more, not imprisoned by those gruelling thoughts and worries grinding me down until the last drop of joy is squeezed out of my life and I'm left with a dry mouth and a knot in my stomach. The decision to take the medication has helped so much to lift the clouds of anxiety that used to swirl around me. And what an eye-opener that's been.

I still have OCD tendencies around my fear of sickness and being unwell, but I'm freer and lighter now. I enjoy things in a way I never could before. I always felt in the past that I had to play down my problems, or keep them secret, apart from telling Chris. But, underneath, my anxiety was physical, like a kind of overdrive. When it flared up, it could disrupt my whole day, completely exhausting me, and I don't think I ever felt fully relaxed. I really did inhabit a world of pain – and it turns out that it didn't have to be that way. It wasn't just 'how I am', or something I had to put up with. There was another choice: to find a way to live my life rather than go on feeling bad, trying to cope, somehow riding it out.

I spent the best years of my life crippled with worries and fears about being away from home and being sick. I wouldn't try friends' cocktails in case they passed their germs to me. Holidays were a hell of anxiety – I never enjoyed a single day and I spoiled so many precious memories with loved ones. The list of wasted time and wasted happiness feels so gloomy that it's hard to think about too much.

Instead of countless anxieties to battle every day – as I had for the last twenty years – now I've been left with only one. I want to heal the sadness I feel at wasting so much of my life overwhelmed by worry. Perhaps it's the next challenge I face. I also find it strange that it was a terrible global health emergency that finally brought me to a point at which my anxiety could be treated. Perhaps when everyone else was suddenly so frightened of infection, it made my fears feel valid – valid enough to ask for help at last.

Chief Shepherdess

Sorry, ladies, gonna have to bail. The ewes have got out on the road. Love u xoxo.

Drinks and dinner with the girls are off the cards. Again. I hastily tap a WhatsApp message, then push my feet into my wellies and shuffle towards the door while I pull my overalls over my shoulders. I love my friends dearly but there's no way on earth that I'll have the energy for a conversation with anyone after rounding up Herdwicks on the Downs. I won't be having dinner now, so I grab a banana and zip up my fleece, yanking a stray lock of hair that's got stuck in the zip and suddenly realizing why there has been so much hair breakage since my career change. A few minutes later, I'm heading along the A20.

Twenty-four hours a day, 365 days a year, we're at the beck and call of creatures that take great pleasure in anything mischievous or causing as much inconvenience as they possibly can. The unspoken rule is never to utter the words: 'I'm going to take it easy this afternoon.' Don't even let the thought enter your head. And definitely don't let the goats hear you say you want a little lie-in. You can bet your bottom dollar that that's when you'll get a Facebook message from a concerned rambler that 'the little grey goat' has its head stuck in the fence or a lamb has got out onto the road.

Every day we're one misjudgement from injury or even from disaster, from being run over to being crushed by a trailer. The scariest near-miss I've had was last year when two goat kids in the pet pen, Mary-Kate and Ashley, tried to jump out and knocked over the heat lamp. I wasn't there, and by the time I got back there was a patch of smouldering embers as big as a dinner plate and growing. Fortunately, the kids had run away, but that barn is full of bales of straw and Compass Corona. The heat lamp should have been somewhere safer, and just one moment's inattention might have had horrific consequences. All we can do is make sure to get enough sleep so that we don't make silly mistakes.

For everything to run smoothly, farming is always first in the calendar – which can make it look like you don't care about the other people in your life. You miss birthday parties. You're regularly late. You cancel arrangements at the last minute. You forget to text back for ten hours. It can drive a wedge into friendships – which has happened to Chris's friends and mine. The result for many farmers can be loneliness, leading to poor mental health, and suicide rates in the farming world are sky high. It's a dark, distressing shadow over the countryside.

Farming is also extremely cool these days and 'farmlife' has become a popular social-media hashtag. It certainly seems to speak to a lot of people. Perhaps it's the pandemic that's made them want to escape from cities, and all those Instagrammed images of the peaceful, idyllic countryside look like a fantasy world. Just type #farmlife into Instagram for your regular daily dose of beautiful sunrises, fit-looking people with grubby hands and banging tan lines, leaning against hay bales, lots of super-cute lambs and cool types dressed in farmer chic, drinking sloe gin at the county show.

I started posting on Instagram as 'The Chief Shepherdess' in October 2018. The idea was that our friends, family and clients could watch us make fools of ourselves while they were sitting in a front-row seat and we scrambled through the most mental career change ever – live on air. At first, uploading our escapades onto the new Instagram page was easy and fun. I also loved being able to offer an escape for people who don't feed baguettes to cattle to start their morning, or have a garden large enough to soak up rays of sun on their lunch break. That's a real pleasure: giving an Access All Areas, VIP pass to those who aren't as fortunate in the nice-views-and-cheeky-animals department as we are.

I used my account to voice the dramas I was going through – and was completely blown away by the response. Suddenly my inbox was glitching at the influx of messages coming through. There was so much encouragement and support. Social media has a terrible reputation as a dark place full of trolls and 'Karens' moaning about the bin men leaving the wheelie two metres too far away. ('Karen' has become a kind of shorthand term for somebody who's over-critical and demanding.) But as with most things, I've learned that it is what you make it. The energy you put out into the world comes right back at you.

The Chief Shepherdess account began to grow. Just as money comes to money, so fame is drawn to fame. Instagram success is all about who you hang around with or who 'tags' you in posts and stories. And once you get a shout-out from a media personality, you're away: your follower count jumps up. For me, it was DJ Greg James on his Radio 1 show. He mentioned my name and my Instagram page and reshared a little video I'd made of Indie licking milk off a lamb's face. It was a positive, light-hearted story when so many people were listening to the radio for reassurance during the early stages of the pandemic, and it certainly struck a chord with his audience. A friend of mine rang me and told me what Greg James had said, but when I tried to look on my phone to check the responses, I couldn't. There were so many it had crashed my Instagram. I remember standing out there in the field just staring at the screen and thinking, *Wow. This is just too wild.*

The Chief Shepherdess had taken off. When I hit the ten-thousand-followers mark, the brands came in, with requests to promote anything and everything. Sounds great, right? But it's the point where your integrity is at risk of taking a plunge down. All of a sudden I had budget production-company admin assistants sending me messages – after following me for a hot five seconds – confessing their undying admiration for my 'journey' and asking if I'd like to feature in a brain-dead new TV show. Or a fast-fashion line would reach out with messages saying, 'We just love your page! Your aesthetic and values are really in line with ours!' *Well,* I was tempted to reply, *not so much, since you're pushing cheap crop tops. I'm honestly struggling to see how we connect.* But that's how they get you, and before you even know it, you're advertising polyester hoodies made in a sweatshop located in a developing country, even though your online biography says #savetheplanet. As for admiring my 'journey' (a term I truly despise), all they wanted was a story of a townie who fell in love with a farmer and lived happily ever after. So flawless. Such a cliché. Such a fake.

That name, though. The Chief Shepherdess. I know

it started off as Chris's jokey nickname for me, but it sounds pretty confident, right? The queen of having her shit together. Except that's not how it is. The string of events leading to the present day has been far from flawless – quite the opposite. Flawed. But beautifully so. Chris will accuse me of being a drama queen here, but we have struggled and still struggle. I honestly thought my greatest challenge would be trying to lead a champagne lifestyle on a lemonade budget (which has to be one of my all-time favourite sayings!). Instead, I've found a place in the world that's meaningful and real.

The brands don't want that, though. They're so transparent. They don't even look at what I'm saying: my words are irrelevant. All they see is the little number at the top of the page: my followers. And the bigger that score, the harder it becomes to work out who's really a pal and who's creeping around you to feed off your page and grow their own number. That was when I realized I had to make a choice. I could go the social-media-influencer route and make whatever name I could out of that for as long as I was considered to be cool (which I knew wouldn't be very long). Or I could stay with what I'd chosen to be – a farmer. I decided to stick to what felt true.

But the attention was very exciting. A few weeks later, around spring lambing 2020, I was booked to do a photo shoot for a national magazine. My friends were all asking what I'd wear and how I'd have my hair. I didn't have a lot of time. When you have to be up and out at the crack of dawn, you pick your beauty battles. Do I want perfectly winged eyeliner that's going to smear down my cheeks by sunrise? Or do I want to make sure I've got a full belly so I don't crave Maltesers by 10 a.m.? We were mid-lambing, living in the caravan inside a hay barn with a shower that gets three minutes of hot water if we're lucky. Not an ideal location to scrub up for the Oscars. A spritz of face-tanning mist and a hair wash the night before and I was hot to trot.

I also felt a responsibility to the people who'd be looking at the article. There's enough pressure on young girls to worry about their appearance, exactly like I used to do. Did I want them thinking that farming is some glamorous scene where we lounge around on hay bales looking flawless? (Mind you, I did go on to feature in the *Daily Mail* in a ballgown and heels, holding a cute lamb. But I'm pretty certain nobody thought that was realistic!)

I know exactly how all those girls looking at social media feel. I never used to be seen dead – even in the supermarket – without at least a touch of bronzer, and it's taken me quite a while to feel confident barefaced. This is where working out of doors in the countryside – all that fresh air and vitamin D – has given me some pretty big advantages. My skin doesn't look tired any more. I've saved a fortune in face cream, and I don't need a full face of make-up to feel alive or disguise the previous night's antics and deep-set eye bags.

Inner acceptance of my appearance wasn't a big feminist epiphany for me. It simply stemmed from always being in a hurry. Now it's grown into so much more than that. It's the confidence to know that even when I haven't brushed my hair in five days and it's been in this dreadlocked bun for three and I'm not sure if that's a tan line or a dirt line you can see, and I stink like an actual pig pen – well, so what? I still have my gold hoops in and a smile on my face – and *that's* the part that matters.

I wish I could teleport back in time and tell myself this (not that teenage Zoë would have listened). When you've been to a tiny village primary school where everyone lives in each others' pockets, a bitchy all-girls grammar school, and an art college where everyone pretends to be free-spirited (they aren't), and finally lived in a fashion-conscious city like London while working in hairdressing, the freedom from pressure to look a certain way takes some getting used to. Hitting puberty at school was harrowing and I spent every waking hour comparing every detail of my appearance to everybody else's. *Why isn't my hair sleek and poker straight? Why can't I get some GHDs – those very high-end hair-straighteners – for Christmas? Why do I have so many moles, like a dot-to-dot puzzle made out of Coco Pops? Why won't Mum and Dad let me wear thongs from La Senza?*

I spent years in that pale blue school-uniform blouse refusing to put my hand up and answer questions in class in case I had sweat patches. I dumbed myself down and refused to thrive because I was scared to show I had perspired, which is a normal bodily function. Sweat patches for me now are a medal for a job well done and a symbol of all those calories I've just burned off – not to mention Reason Number 260 why I don't need a gym membership now that I'm a farmer.

Times are certainly changing. I'm not too sure who decides what's 'in fashion' but I definitely want to thank them for making farming cool again. Now the farmer's kids at school won't be picked on for being 'trampy' because they have straw in their hair. Other kids might even be envious that they spend weekends out on the quad bike. It's cool to be different, and hallelujah for that.

* * *

'Hey, Zoë!' I heard my mate (and former hairdressing client) Fiona on voicemail. 'This will sound a bit out there, I know, but I've got a photo shoot coming up and – um – I was wondering if you could let me borrow a lamb to use as a prop?'

I rang her back at once. Fiona's job is to source locations and equipment for big companies and this shoot was for a *very* upmarket fashion designer who was launching a range of children's clothes. She'd arranged to use a gorgeous walled garden, and a week or so later, I set off in my 4 x 4 with Norma the pet lamb sitting next to me on the front seat. When I arrived, the team was setting up and it was pretty familiar: back in my hairdressing days, I'd done work like this with photographers, styling assistants and reflective umbrellas everywhere to soften the light. It looked like fun – just like old times.

I'd given Norma a pep talk in the car but I didn't have any concerns about how she would behave. I'd picked her because she was an orphan, hand-reared, very friendly, and she usually just followed me around. But the second she saw all the lights-camera-action going on, she went absolutely hyper, bolting round the garden like a kid that's OD'd on Smarties. The three little girls modelling the designer clothes looked incredibly cute in their floral dresses and frilly socks. The idea was that they would sit on the grass with Norma in their arms and stroke her. But I couldn't even catch her.

'Ha-ha-ha! You know what they say! Don't work with animals and children!' the photographer told me. Everyone laughed politely, but a few minutes later when Norma was still dashing up and down and I was chasing after her making sheep noises – which the kids thought was hysterical – he tried the same joke again and nobody cracked a smile.

I was sweating with the stress by now. I could feel the trickles running down my back under my T-shirt. Finally, I got Norma into position, but she wouldn't stop wriggling about and kept trying to eat all the little girls' flowers. We managed to get a few nice shots – result! – and then they had to change the children's outfits and do the set-up all over again.

At that point, a member of the team, naturally dressed from head to toe in clothes made by the designer, offered to hold Norma. She seemed keen on this idea – Norma was adorable after all – and things were calmer by now. I thought it would be okay and handed her over. But after we'd been chatting for a minute or two, she suddenly cried, 'Oh, my God! I think your lamb just pooed in my pocket!' While Norma was snuggling up to her ever so cutely, she'd managed to drop a nugget straight down.

Mayhem. The children were screaming with laughter. There was sheep shit all over the woman's mobile phone and bits of it stuck underneath her nails and she was trying to pretend that she didn't mind about the mess on her very expensive jacket. I was mortified. It was the end of Norma's media career. Two worlds collided that day, for sure, and I definitely knew which one was mine.

* * *

By now I'd built up quite an Instagram girl gang. It had become a part of my life – and still is: chatting away with friends, sharing our daily trials and tribulations, however gory or heartbreaking. But I was also finding out that this kind of fame has some pretty big downsides.

First of all, I'm part of big business, just like everyone who goes on social media. I'm constantly aware that

I'm playing into Mark Zuckerberg's hands – and his bulging wallet – by showing up on Insta every day, posting videos of goats burrowing under a gate to *The Great Escape* theme tune.

Then there's the content I put out. I'm not particularly filtered or curated on Instagram. Some may call what I do oversharing. My feed could be a goat sticking its tongue out, and two stories later it could be Chris's face superimposed onto a video of *Rambo*. Completely random – but also completely unique and personal. So that means I'll use swear words, or I'll show photos of dilated sheep vulvas with the caption #vagwatch, or I'll upload a video of a billy goat licking his penis and drinking his own urine. The majority of my videos would be suitable for children (if the volume was off) but it's Russian roulette: you never know what I might post in the next slide. I'm more than comfortable with this. I won't censor my personality just because I have tens of thousands of people watching. What's the Golden Rule? *You do you, babe.*

Still – with my small segment of the internet comes influence and power. And back-stabbing and resentment sit right alongside them. Navigating the social-media minefield turned out to be exhausting. I've been cyber-bullied because of the number of followers I have. I've faced criticism for the way I speak, for showing a maggot-ravaged carcass being put in the dead bin, for using Indie's rope lead in an emergency to help deliver a calf that was stuck, and because I once shared a story I was told by a paramedic who was called to a house where a man had a bedpost stuck up his arse. For doing this, I've been accused of being a disgrace to the farming industry and unfit to be an ambassador for it.

And that's what they're missing. I never signed up to be an ambassador for an entire industry! And, naturally, it upset me at first because I'm human, vulnerable – and who enjoys being the subject of an online pile-on? But the only possible response – of course – was that I decided to stop giving a fuck. It was the best thing I ever did. That – and a huge cull of people I followed. If something shitty happened to me – like being bullied – I openly asked if anyone else had had something similar going on. Most importantly, I tried to stay unapologetically true to myself. This might mean I wouldn't get gifted free quad bikes, or be approached by global brands, but at least now I knew that the approaches that came my way were authentic.

Looking back, I wish I'd called out the cyber-bullies straight away. At the time, I wasn't strong enough to do it. I thought my overactive, sensitive mind was playing tricks on me and I was partly to blame for what was going on. I should have realized that the cause of what was happening was jealousy and fear of being outshone. But at the time, I wasn't secure enough in myself to say, 'Enough is enough. I will not be treated like this.' When we think of bullying, we think about kids in primary school. But social media, unfortunately, enables bullies to feel brave and powerful enough behind their keyboards to flex their cowardly muscles.

* * *

OMG, hun, living your best life #couplegoals

This comment pinged up on my Instagram not so long ago. The comment was far from reality. We were two weeks into lambing. It was freezing and damp and relentlessly miserable. I was struggling emotionally and living in a fifteen-foot caravan, which had a carpet of hay, no matter how many times I swept the floor. I was far from living my best life, and my boyfriend and I were so worn out that some days we felt like dismembering one another using the most barbaric methods possible.

That user who commented on the post, like many of my other followers, saw me in a *very* idealized way. But as more and more 'farm influencers' have started to chase Instagram fame, I've noticed the gap getting wider between real-life on-the-ground farming and what appears online. Their stories have become increasingly rehearsed and the content is less reality-based and more polished. Constant mud and unfair pork prices might damage your mental health, but they're not nearly as harmful as the sight of picture-perfect farmyards and glossy-haired girls in impossibly clean wellies, setting beauty standards you've no chance of reaching. If you let yourself buy into that kind of image, social media really can be bad for you.

I was loading the truck with some square bales of hay when a clapped-out pick-up truck drove up the track into the yard. As I walked over, the man at the wheel rolled down the window and asked me, 'All right, love? Is the farmer about?'

Once again, I internally rolled my eyes.

'Yeah. How can I help you?'

There was a short pause before he stuttered, 'Ah. Um. I've just come to buy some hay.'

I've lost count of the number of times I've been asked this question. I just don't look like Old MacDonald. I'm too young. I'm most likely wearing earrings. Above all, I'm a woman. No one is trying to insult me, and it doesn't even wind me up any more. I think it's exactly the same as when you're told that your hairdresser's name is going to be Charlie: you think, *Okay – that's short for Charlotte, right?* and this forms the expectation of the person you imagine you're going to see. You don't think 'short for Charles'. The older generations are accustomed to certain genders fulfilling certain roles, and getting upset about it is not worth the bother. Point it out to them, okay, but it's hard to change people when they've known things a certain way for a very long time.

All we can do is strive to make these stereotypes less prominent for the next generation. If you're visiting a farm, there ought to be somewhere for you to change your tampon. That should be normal. If I'm lucky enough to have children, I don't want them to be fazed when they see a Black farmer on telly, or to bat an eyelid if a woman is breastfeeding her baby while standing at a livestock auction.

For now, farmers like me are using hashtags like #womeninag and #femalefarmer. They're doing it to fight for a voice and to stand strong with one another in this community of like-minded individuals all over the country. I'm proud of the women around the globe who are breaking barriers still in place from centuries ago (what's taken us so long?) and channelling the power of the Land Girls who did much of the farm work during the Second World War – while so many men were away fighting – and kept Britain fed. Just like them, I'm a woman and I'm capable. I can do my bit for farming just by showing up and being a female farmer.

I also feel that I'm part of a wave of change in agriculture, and it's incredibly exciting. In June 2022 I went to Groundswell, a regenerative farming conference held in Hertfordshire. It's the sort of thing Chris loves – it's run by farmers, for farmers. The community can exchange knowledge, ideas, and learn more about conservation agriculture and soil health. I thought it sounded fun too, and that it would be a chance for me to meet some of the people I often chat to over social media. I was expecting to have a few drinks, mix and mingle.

Groundswell turned out to be far more than this. There was a real festival vibe, with women breastfeeding around the place. Everyone was chill and I felt truly accepted and very comfortable in my skin. All the attendees wore a lanyard with a label round their neck. (Mine read *Zoë Colville, Farmer, The Little Farm Fridge.*) It was liberating to see that no one questioned this, or even looked twice: the first question whenever I was meeting someone new was just 'What do you farm?'

I remembered how, at the beginning of my farming life, I'd felt uncomfortable and out of place in a little livestock market. Now here I was at a national event, standing at the bar (in leopard-print shorts and pink Crocs because, always remember, *You do you*) talking to soil scientists and researchers, who send robots out into the fields to test soil quality. It's a true sign of the times.

Our industry needs new thinking. It's only a few years since the Brexit referendum plunged the whole agricultural community into uncertainty. There were many arguments going on, and far more questions than answers. Farmers' gatherings and online forums vibrated with earnest discussions about loss of subsidies and trade deals. Would the lamb price fall through the floor? Would the financial structures the industry has depended on for many years all be scrapped? We need to talk about the future of our industry, the challenges it faces and the possible solutions we can come up with. Many farmers these days are seriously ahead of the times with their practices, educating the rest of us slowcoaches in how bright the future could look and the changes that are needed to bring it about. Groundswell seemed like the kind of place where the new thinking will happen.

I also felt I'd earned my place there. I used to get upset if someone gave me crap on Instagram because they'd spotted that one of my goats didn't have an ear tag, but now I own my right to be at an event like that, playing a part in understanding the science behind food production. It boosts my confidence.

At one point I was on my hands and knees in a field – with a G&T in one hand – rifling through cow shit while a woman I follow on Insta was teaching me about dung beetles and how to aerate the soil. That evening I was chatting in the loo with a social-media friend who runs an organic dairy in the West Country – I'd never met her in person until then and I soon realized that if we actually hung out together, we'd be close. The whole scene felt surreal. It was like being back in a sticky-floored club toilet in London, except that now this bonding was happening at a soil convention, in a Portaloo. I buzzed, accepting that my life had come full circle and I was totally invested in this. I still am.

* * *

How's Frankie doing now?
  Did he make it?
  Hang in there, Frankie!
  Is he okay?
  Please don't die, Frankie!
The messages of concern and good wishes were piling

up in my Instagram account. Frankie, a Hebridean cross Southdown lamb, fluffy as you like, had been handed to me by Chris in a bucket seemingly dead, his head rolled back at an angle worthy of *The Exorcist*. Saliva was pouring out of the corners of his mouth – 'watery mouth', which usually means an E. coli infection. I slipped on my gloves and injected a millilitre of antibiotic into his leg muscle. E. coli is a bacterial infection, which you have to take control of as fast as you can – the bacteria multiply so unbelievably quickly. Then into the lamb oven he went, until his mouth wasn't cold any more and the saliva wasn't stringy. I thought there was a chance now. Hopefully, he'd be well enough to hold up his head in good time so that I could feed him some colostrum. I put a quick pic of him on Instagram then went about my business.

He got a huge reaction – not surprising, really, given his cuteness. A few hours later, I saw on my phone that he'd captured twenty thousand hearts and had shedloads of messages wishing him well. This was lovely, but also quite a worry. What if I had to break bad news to his fans? Praying that he hadn't taken a turn for the worse, I rang Chris.

'How's the little lamb in the oven, babe?'

'You mean ol' Frankenstein?'

'Frankenstein?'

'Yeah. He's coming to life!'

And he was. That was how he got his name. When I opened the lid of the lamb oven, Frankie the Insta ram was practically standing on his feet. I felt a massive rush of relief. I tube-fed him his first colostrum, but by the second feed he took it out of the bottle, like a champ. It's such a moment of triumph when they do that, and really shows some fight. I'll never get bored of the feeling I get when they master how to suckle: something clicks inside them and instinct kicks in. He went from strength to strength, his fan group showing he'd become a huge hit on my page.

Frankie's still with us, running around like a freeloader on our best grass. One of the best things about working for yourself is that you can call the shots. If there's a special soul that you bond with, you can keep him or her. He was hardly our best breeding stock, but too sickly to castrate, so by the time he was strong enough it was too late to put a band on his nuts and he kept them, much to Chris's dismay. That meant he had to stay separate from the young females so he didn't cause any teen pregnancies. He's just one protein-shake advert away from a trip to Turkey to get his teeth done (sheesh – Chigwell with the boys on a Saturday and wearing no socks with loafers, we all know the type), a fabulous, randy but charismatic Insta-star. I wonder what he'd say if he knew.

* * *

When I worked in London, I was surrounded by people who took great pride in how they looked. Whether their inspiration was Kate Moss or Pete Doherty, they thought very carefully about how they dressed. Farmers, on the other hand, give zero shits. Fewer, in fact. They're the most accepting community in terms of appearance. Chris, for example, doesn't care if there is a rip in the arse of his jeans: he's flashed on Instagram before. He wears pretty much the same thing every single day. Levi's, plain T-shirt (must fit exceptionally well) and knitted jumper from a supermarket (he has the same one in a few colours). The only thing he's picky about is that his hair isn't too long over his ears because 'it tickles', but other than that he's sweet with whatever.

Oh, to be Chris. I don't mind being dirty, mucky, grubby, but I want to feel like I still have something of the flair of my old self. I've had to let go of enough. My perfectly manicured almond-shaped acrylic nails. My MAC lipstick. Even my heated rollers. My Soho pals would have a field day ripping apart my wardrobe choices because work boots ain't pretty and my bum isn't ever perfectly peachy enough.

So: today's OOTD (outfit of the day) is thick woollen socks, my Muck Boot wellies, thermal leggings and long-sleeve top (Marks & Spencer's are the best), roll-neck jumper, leopard-print puffer jacket, child's ski dungarees from Zara, gold hoop earrings and a lime green beret, with my auburn untameable hair cascading out from underneath. Few coats of fake tan and a slick of lip balm. Mud freckles – model's own. We call it 'farm chic'.

I feel good. I'm free of the shackles I've worn my whole life, forcing me to look and to dress in a certain way. There will be no judgement and, safe to say, it's been quite an adjustment but I've reached my destination. Some never do and so I feel eternally thankful. I often wonder if I still lived and worked in the city how I'd be. Would growing older have helped me not to worry about what other people think? Or does my freedom come from completely stripping back my life and starting from scratch – new place, new boyfriend, new skills, no boundaries, no expectations?

I can't imagine I could ever feel this free while I had a boss on my case, and a strict salon schedule with customers arriving every forty-five minutes. Back then, everywhere I went I had to carry my handbag, my Oyster card, my keys. I had to dress in a certain way, and always in clean clothes. What's special about my life now is that we're just living. Every single day means doing what needs to be done: you can't pre-plan. No expectations. Get on with it. Just living.

* * *

To outsiders, our life might look simple. I'm Felicity Kendal from the TV show *The Good Life* with my dungarees and rosy cheeks, picking up windfall apples in the orchard for my pigs while Chris is building a new hay rack for the goats, playing with cute fluffy lambs, driving tractors, making sure everyone is fed and watered, then home for tea and toast.

But our hay racks are all built from scrap because we can't afford new ones. We eat most of our meals on the go. We don't have a tractor so we have to get creative or use a good old-fashioned spade and – just in case you'd forgotten – any sheep's main aim is to die. And yet Chris and I are very rich in life. We don't have to answer to anyone and there is nothing we can't take on if we think it's worth a try.

Motivation-speak can get a bit corny, these days ('Think the unthinkable!'; 'Manifest your dreams!'), but I don't mean it like that. What we've managed to do already is fairly unthinkable – but here we are anyway. We've been faced with real struggles, some that people twice our age haven't faced and never will. Yet our spirits have not been dampened. In fact, with every knock we take, the fire in us seems to ignite once more and burn fiercely.

Another passion that's growing for me is education. The whole idea of going on social media in the first place was to document what we're up to. I never thought about a plan of action or an agenda – I would simply post what came into my head, and if someone living a very different life learned something about farming, that was a bonus. Or if it offered escapism for someone who needed it, that was a bigger bonus.

I think more about what I'm doing now. I know that social media can have a huge impact, positive or negative. I want to use it in the most positive way I can by connecting with children. I don't believe there's nearly enough in the national curriculum for them to learn about how food is produced. In a world full of Kardashians, *Love Islanders* wearing hair extensions that aren't necessarily ethically sourced, and private-jetting, fossil-fuel-burning Formula One racing drivers telling us all to go vegan, I want to use my public profile to make producing food cool.

What do kids love most? iPads, animals and poo – so I'm planning to combine all those three. I'm putting on my education hat and starting a YouTube channel. It will be separate from my Instagram account – so no swearing – and completely child-friendly. I'm going to start small with a weekly ten- or fifteen-minute video, giving bite-sized chunks of information. If we begin like that, perhaps we can build up to the point where kids learn that chickens don't start off in batter – and used to have feathers.

It might just catch on, and if I don't try, how will I ever know? If there ever was a time, it must be now. The pop star Ed Sheeran's buying a farm to rewild. Mrs Hinch, a major celebrity influencer, is at it too. With all that going on, I reckon I've got a fighting chance.

* * *

The first few times Chris had to put an animal out of its misery in my presence, he told me to cover my ears. I covered my eyes as well, and if I could have, I would have removed myself from the entire situation. But, gradually, something changed.

Sheep can't vocalize their feelings, and knowing when any animal is suffering can be a guessing game. Before too long, though, you learn the signs: body hunched over, teeth grinding, standing alone. You also get to know when you can help and when there's nothing more you can do. I wouldn't say that my brain has become accustomed to death, but as I naturally grew in my job and became more committed to the animals, I realized it was important to be a part of their entire journey, and that included their deaths. I owe it to them.

But the sight of death will never be pleasant, and deeply distressing things can happen. One of the worst was shearing day a year ago, on a humid morning in late July with the smell of summer rain in the air. The previous night we'd brought the ewes into the shed so that their fleeces would be dry for the shearers. The first thing we'd intended to do in the morning was get them penned and ready. Their lambs were in a separate field by now, just across the way.

Shearing is a physically exhausting activity: you finish up sweaty, grubby, stinky, and aching in muscles you didn't know you could use. We were gearing ourselves up, eating our second breakfast for energy, when we looked across into their field and noticed one of the lambs leaning against a tree. She was panting heavily, just like a dog, with her tongue hanging out – a behaviour unusual in sheep. She was also drooling green slime from the corners of her mouth.

Chris said he'd take a look and set out across the field. I carried on moving the metal panels we use to build our pens, still getting ready for the shearers. When I saw him striding back, I immediately knew that something was seriously wrong.

'They've been poisoned,' he said to me.

'They? Christ, how many?'

'Five. I can't fucking believe it. I'll go and get them. Can you make another pen? And call the vet.'

He jumped into the truck and drove off across the field, towing the trailer. A few minutes later he was back – and pure carnage came with him. One of the lambs was standing screaming like something from a horror film. Another had flopped onto the ground and was writhing. Sheep aren't vocal about pain and I'd never heard one make a sound like that – even a ewe in the most difficult lambing. Hearing it felt like being punched in the stomach.

'Get them into the pen, Zo.'

When an animal has eaten something toxic, you don't have a long time to act before it's too late. We keep activated charcoal and teabags in the truck: the caffeine in the tea speeds up the heart rate and can boost the circulation to help with the removal of the toxins. It might only make a small difference – but this was a horrible emergency and we had to try whatever we could.

In any crisis, I attend to the details of the nursing and Chris looks at the bigger picture: he was already trying to work out what was causing this disaster. 'We need to know what the hell it is,' he said to me. 'What have they eaten?'

We were working together in the chaos, barely needing to say more. I remembered how I used to watch him when I was very new to farming, amazed that he could anticipate just how an animal would behave and which direction it would run. Now I have that knowledge too.

We got the five penned, drenched them with black tea and gave them all some pain relief. At that point, they were biting at their sides in distress and taking turns to let out the most godawful shrieks. There's something panicky about being close to a living being that's in terrible pain, and I was sobbing while I worked, just trying to do everything I could. I ran back to the truck to get a clean needle and syringe. By the time I got back, one of the lambs was dead.

'Right,' Chris said. 'Only one way to find out what's going on'. He cut into the stomach of the dead lamb. Inside we found a load of mushed-up leaves I didn't recognize. Chris, on the other hand, took one glance then yelled, 'For fuck's sake!' He jumped up and marched off without a word around the perimeter of the field where the sheep had been grazing. A few moments later he stormed back with a plant clutched in his hand.

'Japonica!' he shouted. 'Fucking japonica!' Somebody

had thrown a garden plant they no longer needed (I could see the Pieris japonica label from the garden centre still attached to its stem) over the fence into the field. It must have looked so tempting and the lambs had munched away – but for them (and for goats, also dogs) japonica is deadly poisonous. Whoever had dumped it there, in the middle of the countryside and near livestock, had simply not bothered to find this out.

We did all we could to help but our lambs were still writhing in agony on the ground in front of us. After two more had died, we made the painful decision to end the others' suffering. The vet was on the phone and she agreed that we had no choice. In one fell swoop we'd lost five lives, simply due to someone's ignorance.

The ribbons of life and death weave through my life daily. I'm so different from the Zoë who once used clothes, booze and distractions because she was afraid to look deeply within. I know there are no guarantees. I don't naively take it as a given that there will be life tomorrow. A lamb might struggle to be born, then fail to take its first breath. I know that the green shoots may not sprout in March, and accept that the cycle of life and Nature meant that my dad didn't live to be a grandpa.

I still carry the grief of losing him. Sometimes it feels a bit like swimming in a dark and awful sea where the animals around me have become my helpers and Nature is the lifeguard, teaching me when I need to kick a bit harder to stay afloat. It's fucking grim to hurt so much that you don't recognize yourself, or to live with the memory of watching the life drain from the eyes of someone you love. It's also painful to end a living creature's existence with your own hands.

But it's the bittersweet price I pay for being privy to an uncut version of reality. As a farmer, I've got myself a VIP seat to the rawest, grittiest, downright realest show of all time. And new life comes when you truly need it. Mother Nature's got your back, bitch.

Acknowledgements

First things first. I want to raise my glass to the absolute babe that is Liz Sheppard. For helping me shape and mould the jumbled, messy fifty-thousand words I'd written into a structured piece of writing that actually reads like a book worthy to be read by more than just my Grandpa Tim. Piecing together anecdotes, handwritten diary entries and 3 a.m. voicenotes to myself was no mean feat, but I think we've done it. And facetiming me sitting on the barn floor with a dodgy signal, while you tried to work out a way to liken shearers to *Magic Mike* and tried to understand what a vaginal and rectal prolapse looks like with various Google images was a challenge that you took in your stride. Although our relationship was fairly short, you know more secrets about me than my therapist and that's a testament to your character. Cheers to you!

Cheers to you, Mum, for keeping the secret about me writing a book even though I could see the pride spilling out of you every time we had distanced dog walks at the farm. I wish Dad could see how independent you've become – motorway driving and DIY solo. A force to be reckoned with! Hols and I will drink to that.

Next up, Chris Woodhead. Thanks for finding the balls to message me and ask me on a date, even if you needed some Dutch courage first. We live a wild life, but we're pretty fuckin' cool for sticking at it.

Charlie Campbell for guiding me through this foreign and frankly downright intimidating process, with your wealth of knowledge and reassuring manner. I knew from day one when I spoke to you in the dark depths of lockdown that your soothing, experienced voice would be the one I'd need most during this whole out-of-body experience.

And finally, all at Penguin Random House, past and present. Eloisa, Danai, Kate, Sally, Viv, Rosie and the rest of the Chief gang. One last shoutout to Lizzy – for sending me that email many moons ago when I was at my lowest and giving me something to focus on even though I never truly believed I would pull it off. I guess the fact I'm writing this, be it on my phone in the truck at 9 p.m., filthy dirty from working sheep all day, with muscles aching, but high on life, means we did it. I'll definitely sink a tequila to that!

About the Author

Zoë Colville is a hairdresser turned shepherdess. In 2015 she left her fast-paced London lifestyle for a simpler life back home in Kent. Since then she has dabbled in both hairdressing and farming side by side. Leaving salon life in 2018, she took the plunge to farm full-time with her partner Chris, using Instagram to vlog their escapades and racking up a rapidly growing following. She has a partnership with the farming brand Muck Boot, and recently featured in *Country Living*'s 'Nature & My Mental Health' video series.